Shape the Future, Lead Like a Pro

3 Skills Every Great Leader Needs to Succeed ... with Authentic Leadership

from GetTheBigYES.com

Tom Marcoux

Spoken Word Strategist

Executive Coach – Pitch Coach

Speaker-Author of 45 books

CEO

A QuickBreakthrough Publishing Edition

Other Books by Tom Marcoux:

- Soar with Confidence: Pitch – Lead – Succeed
- Relax, You Don't Need to Sell (Make Sales without Being Pushy) … with Authentic Marketing
- Dark Arts Defense Against Toxic People
- Darkest Secrets of Charisma
- What the Rich Don't Say about Getting Rich
- Secrets of Awesome Dinner Guests: Walt Disney, Steve Jobs …
- Amazing You … featuring Secrets of Extreme Confidence
- Time Management Secrets the Rich Won't Tell You
- Darkest Secrets of Persuasion and Seduction Masters
- Darkest Secrets of Making a Pitch to the Film / TV Industry

Praise for *Shape the Future, Lead Like a Pro* and Tom Marcoux

• "*Shape the Future, Lead Like a Pro* empowers you with essential leadership skills. Integrity is the foundation of Authentic Leadership. This book helps you lead and retain people who appreciate true leadership and who will excel for your organization." Christopher Salem, host of Sustainable Success Radio Show – ChristopherSalem.com

• "In his work, Tom Marcoux shows you how to be a better communicator, to get people to actually listen to you and believe you, and then act on what you say." – Danek S. Kaus, co-author, *Power Persuasion*

Praise for Tom Marcoux's Other Work:

• "Concerned about networking situations? Get *Relax Your Way Networking*. Success is built on high trust relationships. Master Coach Tom Marcoux reveals secrets to increase your influence."
– Greg S. Reid, Author, *Think and Grow Rich Series*

• "In Tom Marcoux's *Now You See Me*, the powerful and easy-to-use ideas can make a big difference in your business and your personal relationships." – Allen Klein, author of *You Can't Ruin My Day*

• "In *Darkest Secrets of Persuasion and Seduction Masters: How to Protect Yourself and Turn the Power to Good*, learn useful countermeasures to protect you from being darkly manipulated."
– David Barron, co-author, *Power Persuasion*

• "In *Connect*, Tom's advice on how to remain true to yourself and establish authentic rapport with clients is both insightful and reality based. He [shows how] to establish oneself as a credible expert."
- Arthur P. Ciaramicoli, Ed.D., Ph.D., author *The Curse of the Capable*

• "In *Reduce Clutter, Enlarge Your Life*, Marcoux will help you get rid of the physical and mental clutter occupying precious space in your life. You'll reclaim wasted energy, lower your stress, and find time for new opportunities." – Laura Stack, author of *Execution IS the Strategy*

Visit Tom's blogs: GetTheBigYES.com   PitchPowerFest.com
YourBodySoulandProsperity.com

Tom Marcoux

CONTENTS*
* These are highlights. Much more is in this book!

DEDICATION AND ACKNOWLEDGEMENTS

This work is dedicated to YOU. Here are **Special Offers:**

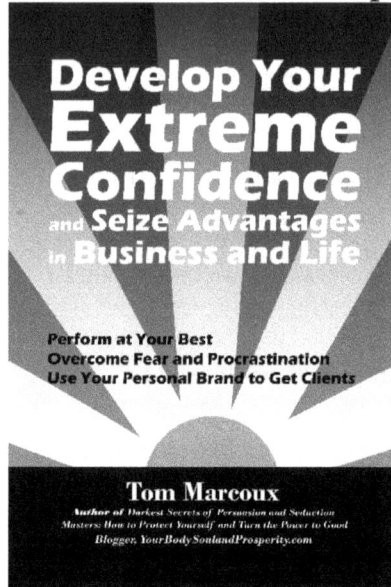

- **Get your free eBook** *Develop Your Extreme Confidence and Seize Advantages in Business and Life* at http://bit.ly/29bVpox

- Apply for a **Free Breakthrough Strategy Session** with Tom Marcoux https://tomsupercoach.com/breakthrough/

This book also dedicated to the terrific book/film consultant, and author Johanna E. Mac Leod. Thanks to Benson Wong for comments. Thanks to Johanna E. Mac Leod for this book's cover. Thanks to my father, Al Marcoux, for his concern and efforts for me … and to my mother, Sumiyo Marcoux, a kind, generous soul. Thank you to Higher Power … and to our readers, audiences, clients, my graduate students and my team members of Tom Marcoux Media, LLC and GetTheBigYES.com. The best to you.

Shape the Future, Lead Like a Pro

"I must be a better leader, or this project will fall apart," my new client, Amanda, said.

"What are you most concerned about?" I asked.

"My team doesn't think we can get out of this tailspin."

"They'll have to *trust you* instead of their first impression," I said. "We'll work to get the best out of you. You'll learn and rehearse—with me—three skills."

"Three?"

I then described *Three Skills every great leader needs to succeed:* **Relate, Optimize and Intuit**.

"Amanda, I'll train you to be a *RoiLeader*. It's time for you to *Shape the Future*." I said.

Amanda knew that ROI refers to "Return on Investment." I emphasized our best investments are in our own skills and into the people we're talking to. I break down **R.O.I as Relate, Optimize and Intuit.** I've coined the term, the RoiLeader. Using these three skills, you become the *trusted* leader. **Let's look at the bottom-line: Your benefits with this book include that you'll become the trusted leader**

who gets team members to be engaged, and innovation and high productivity rise up.

Be the disruptor, not the disrupted. – Dan Burrus, futurist

I take from the Dan's quote that **we cannot be reactive. We need to be proactive.** We'll talk about how to *handle disruption and even get ahead of the upcoming surprises*—later in this book.

"Real artists ship." – Steve Jobs

"It's in our best interest to put some of the old rules aside and create new ones and follow the consumer—what the consumer wants and where the consumer wants to go." – Bob Iger, CEO of The Walt Disney Company

You need to be the cause *not* the effect of marketplace changes. You need to get into the arena, take the right risks and make the big, vital decisions.

It's understood that great leaders are masters of relating and optimizing time and other resources. As I mentioned, R.O.I is Relate, Optimize and *Intuit.*

"Often you have to rely on intuition." – Bill Gates

"Intuition becomes increasingly valuable in the new information society precisely because there is so much data."
– John Naisbitt

"The only real valuable thing is intuition." – Albert Einstein

Many top, successful leaders report that they act on "gut feelings." Researcher and author Gerd Gigerenzer identifies intuition as connected with *data that has not risen to the conscious level.* He notes situations in which a person had a "bad feeling" but could *not* give a persuasive, rational argument. Then the company went ahead into what became a business disaster, and the person's "bad feeling" proved an accurate assessment.

The RoiLeader uses intuitive impressions as part of their toolkit to lead well.

Here's one of my favorite things to say about leadership: *Leadership is about helping your team know what they don't know, see what they can't see and ultimately, they feel empowered to do what they couldn't imagine doing.*

Why Many Leaders Fail—They're Missing One of the Three Key Puzzle Pieces

Some leaders are good with people. Others are good at scheduling and optimizing resources. Still, others are good at making the intuitive calls.

In today's marketplace, **you need all three: Relate, Optimize, Intuit.** That's right: You need to be a *RoiLeader.*

When I teach MBA students on the topic of "Authentic Leadership Communication," I focus on having the students actually *practice* methods within the first 9 minutes of the class. Why? To be an RoiLeader, we need *the experience of what it feels like to truly connect with our communication.*

"The single biggest problem in communication is the illusion that it has taken place." – George Bernard Shaw

Have you had the experience of someone interpreting what you said in the worst way possible?

Maybe you replied with: "Wait. I didn't mean *that!*"

The RoiLeader does *not* leave communication to chance. The RoiLeader checks in with his or her conversation partner. You can find out how well you're communicating by asking a listener, "What did you hear me to say?"

This book is filled with communication secrets that make you into an articulate and *trusted* leader.

RoiLeaders use this following method to get clarification:

You can say something like: "I heard you to say that ___ is most important to you. Do I have that about right?"

The above method helps you check in with your conversation partner.

If you got something wrong, your conversation partner can clarify what they meant.

Then you can respond with something like: "So, what I heard was …."

To Shape the Future, Use Tools and Processes to Expand Your Thinking

The RoiLeader devotes time and effort to expand his or her thinking …

RoiLeaders Get Ahead of Disruption

RoiLeaders keep their eyes open and pay close attention to both the present and what's coming along.

In his article "Three Ways to Avoid Being Disrupted in an Age of Innovation," Sean Donnelly shared sound advice:

"Don't get greedy.

Focus on the customer.

Keep asking 'What if?'" – Taavet Hinrikus, CEO

In 1975, a Kodak engineer, Steve Sasson, innovated a toaster-sized digital camera. However, Kodak executives did nothing with the technology because of their fear of destroying their core business of selling film.

On the other hand, Japanese company Canon Inc. *moved forward* into developing digital photography.

Writer Sean Donnelly suggests that Kodak, thereby, *failed to focus on their customer.*

Keep Asking 'What if?'

- What if you didn't need to go to a store to rent a video? And what if late fees could be eliminated? … *Netflix disrupts Blockbuster.*
- What if you could get good service and easy access to rides? *Uber disrupts taxi cabs.*
- What if you could browse books on your smartphone and get rapid delivery? *Amazon disrupts Borders bookstore.*

The RoiLeader Faces Disruption, Knowing Steps Can Be Taken

Disruption is coming. It's like the tide or the seasons.

Here's an example: I've gone from teaching MBA students in the classroom to writing and leading online classes. Then I wrote/produced webinars. Why? *Because education keeps transforming.* (I still present to audiences at LinkedIn, Stanford University and other organizations.)

This is my 45th book. I still write books—sometimes before I start teaching a new online class. I devote efforts to *move beyond books.*

"It's a good time to be in the content business though, the branded content business." Bob Iger, CEO of The Walt Disney Company

The Pew Research Center noted, in 2016, that those who read e-books tend to use smartphones (and other multi-purpose devices) rather than dedicated e-readers.

The RoiLeader keeps tabs on what is going on with trends and other details of market research.

The RoiLeader Asks "What If?" and *Listens* at Various Levels of the Organization

Here are related questions:
- What if ___ disrupts our ___?
- How can we expand on thinking on this?
- How can we expand our sources of information and understanding about this?

Ask people who are "on the ground." A classic example of asking people who are "on the front lines" is about a private club that found that some men (members) were stealing the shampoo bottles from the showering facilities.

Some of the managers were talking about perhaps, even installing some form of camera system.

Then someone asked a custodian about his take on the situation. He said simply, "Just take away the caps on the shampoo bottles." His point was that this solution would make taking shampoo bottles too inconvenient.

The RoiLeader Develops the "Disruption-Counterpoint-Expansion" Style of Thinking

As we noted before, Kodak failed to take positive steps in the face of the disruption of digital photography.

With my clients, I use the following "Disruption-Counterpoint-Expansion" pattern.

(We'll use Kodak as an example.)

Disruption –

We make film vs. Digital Photography

Counterpoint –

We help people capture images.

Expansion –

So, we *also* make digital cameras.

Kodak could have continued to make film, and with Expansive Thinking, they could have *added* digital cameras to their product line—in a proactive manner.

Here's another example:

Disruption –
We sell ice vs. refrigeration
Counterpoint –
We keep things cold.
Expansion –
So, we make/sell refrigerators.

When we look at the above, a seller of ice could ask, "How do we get into the refrigeration business?"

Now, here's your chance to practice this "Disruption-Counterpoint-Expansion" Pattern of Thinking.

Exercise #1

Fill in the blanks:

Disruption –

_____ vs. _____

Counterpoint –
We do _____ for people who _____

Expansion –
So, we can add _____
OR

_____

OR

_____

The RoiLeader Embodies Authentic Leadership

When authors and researchers discuss Authentic Leadership, they mention these elements: a) Self-awareness (values and more), b) Relational Transparency (open sharing balanced by a minimization of inappropriate emotions), c) Balanced Processing (listening to opposing viewpoints and delivering fair-minded consideration) and d) Internalized Moral Perspective (holding a positive ethical foundation).*

To begin our conversation about this material, I'll offer some brief comments on each element:

a) **Self-awareness (values and more)**

What is most important to you? Another important aspect is whether you're aware of your own limitations. RoiLeaders hold the value that they will *not* let their personal limitations/weaknesses adversely affect their team and clients/customers. RoiLeaders reflect on their personal journey in terms of their successes, failures, strengths, biases and weaknesses. They realize that trying to do everything is *not* leadership. For example, I have served as art director on numerous projects, but I do *not* devote time to developing my graphic arts skills. I lead team members who have skills and talents far beyond my own.

Exercise #2

In your personal journal, write your answers to these questions:

* *Authentic Leadership has been studied and discussed by many people including Bill George, Fred O. Walumbwa, Bruce J. Avolio, William L. Gardner, and more.*

- What are my personal limitations?
- What are my personal weaknesses?
- Which of my weaknesses need my attention and my efforts to make improvements?
  (For example, if you have poor listening skills, then you can work on material in this book which can help you elevate your listening skills.)
- What details would be best for me to delegate?

b) **Relational Transparency (open sharing balanced by a minimization of inappropriate emotions)**

Can people trust you? We note that in the definition we have both "open sharing" and "minimization of inappropriate emotions." To put this in few words, unbridled sharing of anger and abuse is wrong and such behavior sabotages one's leadership efforts. Have you noticed that you don't trust people who have no control of their anger, fear or upset? Let's continue looking at the point of Relational Transparency. It's the foundation of building trust.

Do people believe what you're saying? We realize that there is an important difference between telling the truth versus allowing oneself to go into an angry rant against a team member. RoiLeaders know that their team members look to them for leadership. *RoiLeaders must lead themselves.* They get appropriate support. An RoiLeader may vent their feelings to their Executive Coach (and I have heard plenty as an Executive Coach) or, perhaps, a therapist. The RoiLeader remembers to serve the team, clients, and organization's objectives. Some authors suggest that an Authentic Leader keeps his or her ego in check.

Exercise #3

In your personal journal, write your answers to these questions:

- Do I do something that causes people to lose trust in me? (examples: chronic lateness, getting abusive while angry …)
- How can I get help to improve my actions, so people deem me trustworthy?

c) **Balanced Processing (listening to opposing viewpoints and delivering fair-minded consideration)**

Can your team members tell you the tough information to hear? Do they trust that you will hear them out and *not* dump blame on them as you get the bad news? Team members consider RoiLeaders as fair-minded. RoiLeaders know that they can make better decisions when team members feel free to give them *all the news* and data from the front lines.

Exercise #4

In your personal journal, write your answers to these questions:

- Do I make a safe environment, so people feel that they can openly propose an idea that disagrees with my first guess?
- What can I do or say to show that I will consider opposing points of view?

d) **Internalized Moral Perspective (holding a positive ethical foundation)**

What are your values that serve people and that your

team members can adopt with commitment? For example, employees of Disneyland relate to the values of Safety, Courtesy, Show and Efficiency. These values provide a safe and joyful experience for Disneyland park visitors. RoiLeaders also hold values including: empowered team members, strong organization, shareholder value, and serving clients/customers. RoiLeaders also develop companies that serve both the community and the environment.

Exercise #5

In your personal journal, write your answers to these questions:

- What do I hold as important (values) that provide true value and respect to customers?
- What do I hold as my values that provide true benefits and respect to team members?
- How do I hold myself and the team as making a contribution to the community and the environment?
- How can I inspire team members to see their work as contributing to a positive mission of service to clients/customers?

Team members, clients, shareholders, vendors and the public can sense one's authenticity as one communicates according to the principles of Authentic Leadership.

Along this line, in other sections of this book, I'll refer to these categories:

a) Self-awareness (values and more)
b) Relational Transparency (open sharing balanced by a minimization of inappropriate emotions)

c) Balanced Processing (listening to opposing viewpoints and delivering fair-minded consideration)
d) Internalized Moral Perspective (holding a positive ethical foundation).

Develop Authentic Leadership Through Rehearsal

In guiding my clients and my classes of MBA students, I have found that examples and case histories make a great impact. Secondly, in my coaching work, I have observed that the strategy *plus* **directed rehearsal** empowers a person to lead well.

"Practice quiets the anxiety that can cloud our mind in a tough moment. When we lack practice [rehearsal], our good intentions often falter. … [We] need the opportunity to practice courage."
– Chip Heath and Dan Heath

The following example arises from my executive coaching work.

Case History of Authentic Leadership
One of my clients, Marina, used Authentic Leadership to work well with her team members.

In leading her company, Marina guided her team members in a first-time, new project—creating a webinar.

To put this into context, such a pre-recorded webinar is similar to a feature film in terms of scripting and the use of evocative images.

One vital part of a webinar is the "special offer" for an online course to conclude the program.

The idea is that the viewer learned valuable insights and strategies and now would like to follow-up the webinar experience by registering for the related online course.

To make the course more enticing, a company offers *bonus material.*

Marina's first idea was to offer $4,000 worth of bonus materials.

Two of her team members said, "Wait a minute. That's more valuable than the course. You say that the online course is a $2,000 value. This doesn't make sense to offer $4,000 in bonus materials."

Marina felt a big resistance to her team members' idea in her gut. She replied, "But if I was buying something—I'd just want more value."

Now, I'll show how Marina's next actions were empowered by the 4 Elements of Authentic Leadership.

[Additionally, Marina was able to access her ability to use the 4 Elements of Authentic Leadership because she had rehearsed her leadership behaviors with me, acting as her Executive Coach.]

1) *Self-awareness (values and more)*

   Marina is aware that she has some fear related to avoiding the perception of her as weak. But her value of making the correct decision is a higher priority. She has an additional value: She prides herself on hiring smart people who know more than she does—in their areas of expertise. Marina had already practiced this phrase to say to her team members. "So, I had a first idea. Still, I want to know more about your ideas and how your thoughts and feelings are leading to your conclusions. I want to listen some more here."

2) *Relational Transparency (open sharing balanced by a minimization of inappropriate emotions)*

   On the inside, Marina felt irritated that her team

members were pushing back against her first idea. Her initial thought was: *"My idea must be true because I feel it in my gut."*

Because of her sessions with me, Marina was aware that to get the best in innovative ideas and productivity from her team members, she needs to minimize her expression of inappropriate emotions.

So, Marina *avoided* saying the ineffective: "Why are you always giving me resistance?!"

Instead, she took a deep breath and asked, "Is there anything else you want me to know about this?"

3) **Balanced Processing (listening to opposing viewpoints and delivering fair-minded consideration)**
Balance Processing can occur often when we give the ideas some time "to simmer." Marina tells her team members that she'll be thinking about their suggestions that evening.

4) **Internalized Moral Perspective (holding a positive ethical foundation)**
What are the values that make up Marina's Internalized Moral Perspective? She holds to a) serving customers, b) our company is a place where team members can grow, c) my role as leader is to provide the vision and be sure that my own ego does not get in the way.

About two hours later, with a quiet mind, Marina had a shift in her own perspective. She realized that keeping the bonus material as having a smaller value than the actual online course modules sounded "more sensible." She then made the moves of cutting five things from the bonus material and reducing the estimated values of the remaining items. She then praised her team members for holding strong and showing her a new perspective.

The RoiLeader Uses the
Listening-to-Solutions Progression Process

[related to Relational Transparency and Balanced Processing]

"She knows exactly what she wants," is the classic line that top motion picture actors (male and female) say as praise for a feature film director.

Think about it. What defines a good leader?

People express these as good traits:

- Decisive
- Clear in his/her vision
- Good communicator

Let's add *good listener* to the above list.

In her *Fast Company* article "The One Leadership Skill That Impacts Overall Success," writer Lydia Dishman emphasized that being a good listener is a critical skill to develop.

Further, she noted research that expressed: "The top 10 companies on the Global Empathy Index generated 50% more earnings than those ranking least." These Top 10 companies included Microsoft, Facebook, Tesla Motor, and Alphabet (Google). In this case, *empathy* is defined as "the ability to have a cognitive and emotional understanding of others' experiences."

It's vital to realize that the most effective leaders demonstrate empathetic listening skills. It comes down to:

- If the leader doesn't know what they're talking about, you cannot trust them.
- If the leader does not get input from you, you cannot trust them.

Listening-to-Solutions Progression Form

1. One of Your Values

"People will summarize your life in one sentence—Pick it now." – John C. Maxwell

"What I would want people to say about me is, 'I think he had guts.' … I just was built with an innate ability to not let fear guide me in how I run my life." – Bob Iger, CEO of The Walt Disney Company

You as an RoiLeader are meant to provide the vision. Your team desires to know what you want.

They also appreciate how you ask for their input. Still, they want to begin with a leader who provides clear direction.

"This is a very complicated world. It's a very noisy world. And we're not going to get the chance to get people to remember much about us. No company is. So, we have to be really clear on what we want them to know about us." – Steve Jobs

I submit that *being clear about your Core Values is a great start.*

Below I'll talk about the headline. It's a statement of a Core Value that you want to support.

Core values can include: innovation, courtesy, trustworthiness, safety and more.

2. Headline
(sets the topic)

In your "headline," you're providing direction. Here's an example of a headline: "I want to share three ideas about how we can improve our product design process—and streamline our process."

Team members like it when the leader provides real direction.

They comment, "Okay! Now, I know what she wants, and we'll be able to get things done."

However, ineffective leaders neglect to augment their headline with a "tagline."

3. Tagline
(eliciting input from team members)

RoiLeaders know that they get more team member buy-in when they solicit input from team members.

Here's an example of a tagline: "And then, I'll open up our discussion. I'm looking forward to hearing your thoughts, insights and feeling about this."

4. Encourage Input
(avoid "shut downs")

Earlier, I shared that Guy Kawasaki told me that he "was one of the only people to survive working for Steve Jobs twice."

As I mentioned: Steve Jobs was infamous for telling team members: "That's the stupidest idea I've ever heard."

What does that get? Some team members will react by emotionally shutting down. Others react with anger and resentment. Oh, they may keep it hidden. But productivity and innovation are shut down.

"But wait. Apple under Steve Jobs leadership innovated,"

some retort.

One of my friends said, "But what could have Steve Jobs accomplished with *less* 'vinegar'?"

Top leadership thinker Marshall Goldsmith wrote: "What got you here won't get you there. … *Almost everyone I meet is successful because of doing a lot of things right, and almost everyone I meet is successful in spite of some behavior that defies common sense.*"

That's powerful: the idea that people succeed in spite of some counterproductive behavior or bad habit.

On the other hand, I'm suggesting that we respond to people's ideas in ways that encourage input.

Here are examples:

- Interesting
- I'll put that in my soup and stir it.*
- … I'm not sure about that. I'm going to listen some more. What's the advantage of doing it that way?

* I sometimes use this phrase about "soup and stir it" as a brief way to express that I'm going to take the time to think about—and feel my responses—before I dismiss or agree to an idea.

5. Guide Team members to focus on Positive Elements

Here's a valuable question "What does a solution for this look like?" Sure, we can use variations—perhaps, something like: "Let's look at *setting criteria for excellence.* What things need to happen so the consumers think this is an excellent product?"

You're the leader. You set the tone. By saying, "What does the solution for this look like," you affirm that there IS a solution. (I have a phrase: *"Lead so I follow; speak so I believe."*)

24

6. Guide Team members to identify users/ stakeholders and how they might disagree.

Who might object to this possible solution? This is a crucial question. People demonstrate natural doubt and resistance. We need to prepare ahead of time, so we can respond appropriately and effectively to such doubt and resistance.

7. Discover how to get support for the solution

The RoiLeader asks: "How can we get the stakeholders to support this proposed solution?" This is the proactive step. It's time to strategize—together. Creativity is called for. You can also ask, "What's most important to [stakeholder]? And how can we get them *to feel* our solution will support their concerns and values."

8. Set Criteria for Excellence (Agreements)

Who does what, by when – to what level of quality? (What are we agreeing to? You agree to that?)

An Example of Setting Criteria for Excellence

Matt, one of my clients, asked for feedback on his video for members of his esubscribers list. Matt wanted me to send an email that he could view later in the day.

I included this material in my email reply: "I watched the closing of the video. It works. I know you had a couple of stumbles—still, your sincerity came across.

"In another situation, you might try for one more take-- after you've had a chance to rest.

"In situations like this, I *set criteria for excellence.*
- The audience can feel my sincerity
- I got the crucial words in
- I am continuing my momentum

- Nothing is in this project that will cause a loss of credibility

"I've edited so many video performances. And I've directed live theater. No performance arrives as 'perfect.'

Matt, I invite you to:

Check in with your feelings. Did you give them something of value—and did you give it in a way that the audience can take it in?"

Above, I pointed to elements that my client, Mark, could use as benchmarks for Setting Criteria for Excellence.

9. Set Backup Plans for Things turning out as a "bumpy road"

Let's face it together: Fear fills up much of our waking experience.

This book has an extended section about dealing with risk. Things go wrong. Many of us live with a burden of fear each day.

I remember going to grammar school in San Francisco. Several days, I faced violence in grammar schools.

I was in the middle—not a bully and not a "wimp."

I had no idea what the next day would bring. My father, the ex-Marine emphasized: "Fight. Defend yourself. Or you'll get hurt worse."

When my father paid for karate lessons for me, I subsequently had the experiences and skills to defend myself. So, in essence, I had "back up plans for things turning out as 'bump road.'"

"When you're in action, you're focused, and fear is a quiet voice in the background." – Tom Marcoux

Making backup plans and thinking things through is a crucial process.

"In preparing for battle I have always found that plans are useless, but planning is indispensable." – Dwight D. Eisenhower

The RoiLeader realizes that an important part of his or her job is to help team members work with fear, create plans, take appropriate action and assess how things went.

Since there are likely variables out of our control, what are our backup plans when things go wrong and create a bumpy road?

Tania, one of my clients, asked, "What if this marketing plan gains no new clients?"

"I'm glad you brought that up," I replied. "We'll now work on what you can gain from the marketing campaign even if it doesn't yield what you prefer to happen."

Realize:

a) You can't learn how to uniquely market yourself without getting into the arena.

b) If you must justify to someone (a business partner, spouse, someone else) the value of your marketing campaign, get ready to say "This is what I learned…"

c) Use the value of this idea: *"Anything worth doing is worth doing poorly—until you can learn to do it well."–Zig Ziglar*

d) Make your plan build on: "We had a budget for both time and money. We were smart in how we tackled this."

For example, I know a filmmaker who said, "We wanted to do three things with this film: Serve an audience, make progress with our careers and make money. We got two out of three. I know more about how to this. So, I'll make better moves next time."

Years ago, I was part of the team that achieved the milestone "Wells Fargo Bank, the first bank with online banking (1995)." The leader said, "Fail forward fast." We were a team that moved forward as pioneers. Errors and bugs in code would occur. We would fix them!

"Our greatest glory is not in never falling, but in rising every time we fall." – Confucius

"The man who never makes a mistake always takes orders from one who does." – Daisy Bates

"You gain strength, courage, and confidence by every experience in which you really stop to look fear in the face."
– Eleanor Roosevelt

"Inaction breeds doubt and fear. Action breeds confidence and courage. If you want to conquer fear, do not sit home and think about it. Go out and get busy." – Dale Carnegie

"There is no science in creativity. If you don't give yourself room to fail, you won't innovate."
– Bob Iger, CEO of The Walt Disney Company

See the next page for an example of the related form.

Listening-to-Solutions Progression **Form**
(Example)

1. One of Your Values	High productivity
2. Headline (sets the topic)	"I want to share 3 ideas about how we can improve our product design process—and *streamline* our process."
3. Tagline (eliciting input from team members)	And then, I'll open up our discussion. I'm looking forward to hearing **your** thoughts, insights and feelings about this."
4. Encourage Input (avoid "shut downs")	"Interesting … I'll put that in my soup and stir it. … I'm not sure about that. I'm going to listen some more. What's the advantage of doing it that way?
5. Guide Team Members to focus on Positive Elements	What does a solution for this look like?
6. Guide Team members to identify users/ stakeholders and how they might disagree	Who might object to this possible solution?
7. Discover how to get support for the solution	How can we get the stakeholders to support this proposed solution?
8. Set Criteria for Excellence (Agreements)	Who does what, by when—to what level of quality? (What are we agreeing to? So, you agree to that or something else?)
9. Set Backup Plans for Things turning out as a "bumpy road."	Since there are likely variables out of our control, what are our backup plans when things go wrong and create a bumpy road?

© Tom Marcoux Media, LLC   GetTheBigYES.com

RoiLeaders Use Wisdom Related to a "Perception of Being Weak" and a "Perception of Being Strong"

[related to Relational Transparency and Balanced Processing]

Several authors note that poor leadership decisions resulted from leaders getting caught up in their egos and the *fear* of being perceived as weak.

This relates to Relational Transparency as open sharing balanced by a minimization of inappropriate emotions.

When does open sharing often get shut down? When a manager/leader fears being perceived as weak.

For example, as a feature film director, I have experienced times on the set when I really did *not* know what to do next. I was certainly afraid that I might not get all the footage I needed at a filming location.

I could feel my fear rise up. Still, I knew that if I didn't appropriately ask for help, I'd miss out on improving the film with the combined insight of actors and crew people. I had to keep my fear to myself (that is, a bit of "minimization of inappropriate emotions"). It does *not* help to express "I'm scared. Somebody, tell me what to do next."

Since I had been directing films starting at 9 years old, I *had practice* in setting a direction and then asking people to make things better.

Walt Disney called the process "asking people to *plus* the scene." By "plus," he meant add to the value of the scene. He would give bonus money to those people who added a "bit of business" (that's an acting term which refers to some action, some details that were funny) to a scene.

Some time ago, Freida, a friend asked me, "Tom, what has surprised you about leadership or being an executive coach?"

"No one told me how much leadership is about handling fear—your fear and their fear—that is team members, vendors and clients," I replied.

When I say, "handle fear," I mean taking appropriate action and holding an appropriate mindset. I like the phrases: "I'll handle it." Or "I'll take care of it."

Still, it is *not* about eliminating all fear.

My phrase is:

When you're in action, you're focused, and fear is a quiet voice in the background.

In feature filmmaking and theatre, a vital adage is: "Directing is 90% casting." In business leadership, the RoiLeader "casts" and hires the right people and *listens* to them. And then, the RoiLeader can make informed decisions.

"It is better to first get the right people on the bus, the wrong people off the bus, and the right people in the right seats, and then figure out where to drive." – Jim Collins

"It's all about finding and hiring people smarter than you, getting them to join your business and giving them good work, then getting out of the way and trusting them. You have to get out of the way, so you can focus on the bigger vision. That's important, but here is the main thing: You must make them see their work as a mission." – Richard Branson

The RoiLeader must articulate the mission.

The above comment by Richard Branson is one of my favorite quotes because it specifies some of the most vital actions a RoiLeader does.

RoiLeaders Face Fear, Flip It and Forward It

By "face fear, flip it and forward it," I mean identify the fear and then transform it. To use an unusual metaphor. *Find the fear—call it a fire ... and transform it into a springboard.*

Once the fear is a springboard you can "forward it"—that is, move forward or even leap upwards.

The RoiLeader makes sure to surround himself or herself with brilliant people. That's a transformation of the fear of someone else shining brightly next to you.

Years ago, comedian and TV personality Jack Benny said, "I don't care if the guest on my show gets the funny lines. Because people the next day will say *The Jack Benny Show* was funny last night." Jack Benny held the vision that what counted was that his TV show was funny. He didn't let his ego prevent other performers from having their great moments.

If your people are smarter than you, what do you bring to the party? The vision and the willingness to keep your ego out of the way—and make the tough decisions. That's Authentic Leadership.

"The man who never makes a mistake always takes orders from one who does." – Daisy Bates

About the Perception of Being Weak

If team members do not feel safe to bring you the bad news, it's not just a perception ... you would actually be weak.

Strong leaders can take the bad news with a calm

demeanor. Strong leaders make decisions, knowing that some situations can turn out bad and make the leader look bad.

Strong leaders take appropriate risks.

I've heard some individuals suggest: "If I listen too much or I ask for too much input, I'll look weak."

Full stop—now.

"Vulnerability sounds like truth and feels like courage. Truth and courage aren't always comfortable, but they're never weakness." – Brené Brown

Yes, team members want a leader who is strong, who holds the vision when they can't.

They want someone they can trust. If you tell an appropriate detail of your humanness, you set the stage for that vulnerability to sound like truth.

What sounds like an appropriate detail of your humanness? You do NOT confess your dark secret: Team leadership is *not* therapy.

Still, you can make a point, by telling something a bit humorous. Dr. Wayne Dyer warmed up his audiences (later in his career), by telling stories about his teenage daughter putting her hand on her hip and said, "Daaad, you don't know …"

On a few occasions, you can admit your error. It can sound like this. "Sarah, that was a great insight and recommendation. I made a mistake to get caught up in the ____. Sarah, you thought it through and got us to see the underlying problem *and* opportunity. Good work. Thank you."

Here is a vital point. Team members cannot trust a leader who cannot admit personal errors. Why? Because such a leader *cannot* improve!

By the way, admitting one's own error is Relational Transparency.

For example, I have an elderly relative who does *not* admit errors and no one in the family trusts him.

The relative serves as a Reverse Example to me. People don't stand still. Some people do ineffective actions, and they're going in Reverse.

This relative has actually inspired me to be different—to be a good listener and to be a good leader.

Team Members also need a RoiLeader to guide them to focus on Positive Elements.

This makes sense because researchers have noted that human beings have a negativity bias. Think about it. Our ancestors who lived were the ones who identified threats and did something.

Many of us constantly, subconsciously scan for threats.

A RoiLeader is needed to guide us to focus on Positive Elements.

You're perceived as strong with
- Headline
- Guide team members to focus on Positive Elements
- Set Criteria for Excellence
- Hold people to being accountable
- Express Appropriate vulnerability to show you are real and truthful
- Show your awareness of your own "Areas to Improve" and that you are DOING something to Improve.

"The number one certainty in this world is that the future is all about relationships.... All the technology in the world is secondary to interaction between people—constructive, trust-based interaction.... You never want to give people a reason to distrust you." – Dan Burrus

You ARE Strong when you not only face the future—you anticipate the future.

"Be the disruptor, not the disrupted." – Dan Burris

Author and Futurist Dan Burrus writes about Hard Trends. He emphasizes that "a Hard Trend is a future fact that can provide ... certainty."

Here is a Hard Trend: baby boomers are getting older. It's a fact.

Dan Burrus identifies these three Hard Trends: Technology, Demographics and Government Regulations.

I appreciate Dan Burrus' insight. About *Technology*, people will use forms of artificial intelligence to streamline processes. A form of this is revealed in how well Amazon tracks the behavior of their customers.

In terms of *Demographics*, a large segment of the USA population will continue to age.

Government Regulations expand as technology changes citizens' behaviors. We see regulation on the horizon for everything: autonomous vehicles, consumer drones and more.

Dan Burrus also identifies **8 Hard Trend Pathways.** He includes: Dematerialization, Virtualization, Mobility, Intelligence, Networking, Interactivity, Globalization, and Convergence.

Here I'll provide brief comments about the *8 Hard Trend Pathways*.

a) **Dematerialization** – Burrus writes "dematerialization means making things smaller." Consider the various functions people now have in select wrist-devices.

b) **Virtualization** – An example of virtualization is shifting from paper forms to digital forms.

c) **Mobility** – Witness the movement from laptops to wearables (wrist-devices I mentioned above).

d) **Intelligence** – Here's an example: "IBM employees in the U.S. will be able to use Watson supercomputer technology to help find the most effective oncology drugs and clinical trials for their specific cancers, IBM announced." *(Fortune* article by Sy Mukherjee, dated October 11, 2016).

e) **Networking** – Connectivity improves and grows all the time. People wear sensors that monitor their health situations. The data is collected, and it can be transmitted within one's health maintenance organization (HMO).

f) **Interactivity** – Our ability to interact with a product virtually increases rapidly. Want to see real estate property?—take a virtual tour. On Amazon, look at various sections of a book you're considering.

g) **Globalization** – Animated films and TV shows that are designed in the USA and Japan are animated in South Korea. Copies of such shows are streamed on Netflix and sold on Amazon.

h) **Convergence** – Our smartphones serve as prime examples of convergence. We also see convergence among the industries of computers, telecom and entertainment.

None of the above will slow down.

What do we get from all the above? We can consciously choose to open our awareness to these *8 Hard Trend Pathways* that indicate where future disruptions are likely to occur.

"People gravitate to what they believe to be popular... Technology is enabling even more of that."
– Bob Iger, CEO of The Walt Disney Company

Exercise #6:

How can you turn your awareness of the *8 Hard Trend Pathways* to your advantage? (They are: Dematerialization, Virtualization, Mobility, Intelligence, Networking, Interactivity, Globalization, and Convergence.) How can you look to do appropriate expansion? See if you can form appropriate alliances (and be sure to protect yourself from "losing the store").

PART TWO
Relate

The RoiLeader and "Relate" #1

Related to Self-awareness, Relational Transparency, Balanced Processing and Internalized Moral Perspective

The RoiLeader Uses the *Values-to-Message Progression* Process

When I speak of "relate," I'm talking about your relationship to the listener. Even if you talk with someone for five minutes, during such time, you have a form of relationship with that person. More than that, they will remember you and talk about you—which becomes part of your personal brand.

The RoiLeader knows that her personal brand will often precede her before she walks into a room.

Psychiatrist and Professor Robert J. Waldinger of Harvard Medical School notes results of an on-going 77 year-long study of happiness: "The good life is built with good relationships."

In Silicon Valley, where I live, I hear two concepts frequently: disruption and "unfair advantage."

Disruption and values apply to a conversation about Authentic Leadership.

I realize that this above comment may seem unusual.

"Be the disruptor, not the disrupted." – Dan Burrus, futurist

"The best way to predict the future is to create it."
– Peter Drucker

To be the disruptor, you can hold to Core Values and *be flexible in methods.*

Go Deeper and Identify Core Values
Some authors focus on "why?"

There can be a problem with that. *I ask someone why and they jump out of their heart into their head and tell me something that sounds good or at least rational.*

Let's avoid the false data we get. How? We ask "what?"

I ask "what?" in a particular way with *The Five Levels of What.*

Here's an example:

After I gave a speech, an audience member named Clara stepped up to me.

"I need some clarity. I don't know what my next step should be," Clara said, at one point in our conversation.

"In an executive coaching session, I ask a lot of questions and I listen carefully. Let's use an exercise that I call *The Five Levels of What.* Would you like to try this?"

"Yes."

"So, what do you want?" I asked.

"I want my business to be successful."

"What do you get from that?"

"Money."

"Sure, and what do you get from that?"

"I get my son into a good high school. A private school."

"What do you get from that?"

"Freedom from worry. He'll get into a good college."

"What do you get from that?"

"I—I get to feel like I am a good mother."

"So, you want your business to be successful, so you feel like a good mother?" I asked.

She blinked, realizing something important. It wasn't success or money, she really wanted. It was to feel like a good mother. And, it's possible that she wanted to avoid the pain of feeling inadequate or shame related to being a mother.

The Five Levels of What

When we use the Five Levels of What, we can employ questions like:

- What is good about that?
- What does that get you?
- How does that make things get better?
- What does that feel like?

Let's remember that *The Five Levels of What* help us get access to our Core Values.

What can be Core Values?

- Fulfill customers' trust
- Profit
- Value for shareholders
- Support the growth of a team member
- Personal fulfillment
- Serve people
- Innovation
- "Success"
- Build a team that carries forward the value of ____

- create a legacy
- compassion*

A definition of compassion includes: "a feeling of deep sympathy and sorrow for another who is stricken by misfortune, accompanied by a strong desire to alleviate the suffering. (dictionary.com)"

A RoiLeader demonstrates compassion for team members, customers, and herself or himself.

"People will summarize your life in One sentence—Pick it now." – John C. Maxwell

What sentence would you like?

I use the above quote to inspire me to carefully choose what Core Values I focus on.

How about you? What are your Core Values as a leader?

Some leaders say: "Productivity and innovation."

Let's look at Innovation.

What does it get you?

- More value with less resources
- It's exciting
- Achievement: Make a name for yourself
- Leave a legacy
- "Put a dent in the world" – Steve Jobs
- Change history
- Save time [for what?]

Earlier, I mentioned:

- Netflix disrupted Blockbuster.
- Amazon disrupted Borders.
- Uber disrupted taxi cabs.

One might suggest that the above disruptions include *the values of convenience and speed.*

We'll add *"serve people in the way they want to be served."*

For example, my family uses the Amazon Prime process just about every week.

Core Values Can Drive More Profit

In 1965, Van France identified Core Values for Disneyland employees as Safety, Courtesy, Show and Efficiency (which began as "capacity").

Show refers to the whole experience from shopping, dining to rides in Disneyland, which all create an experience like a show (theater/film).

For decades, the Disneyland team members have held to the Core Values and worldwide Disney Parks bring in billions of dollars. For example, in 2016, Walt Disney World earned $4.38 billion.

"Our purpose is hidden in our joy, our inspiration, our excitement. As we act on what shows up in our life our purpose shows up." – James King

Since we're discussing Core Values and Authentic Leadership, let's look at some definitions:
1) *Authentic* is "of undisputed origin; genuine."
2) To *Lead* includes: "organize and direct; initiate action; show someone the way to a destination by going in front of or beside them."
3) *Core Values* "are the fundamental beliefs of a person or organization. These guiding principles dictate behavior and can help people understand the difference between right and wrong." (yourdictionary.com)

Team members and clients want to know that the leader's actions come from an *authentic place.* They wonder if a leader actually has positive values and does care about the people the leader interacts with.

Sometimes people don't say specifically "I like her core values."

But they may say, "I trust Sarah. She's a good team leader. She cares about her people. And, she makes sure we get the most important things done."

The RoiLeader engages in Authentic Leadership. A big part of this is: The RoiLeader "sees the whole chessboard."

We're not reducing the process of leadership to a cold approach to game playing. Let's puts values and heartfelt efforts on the board, too.

To be a great leader, a RoiLeader, you need to devote efforts in these areas: Relate, Optimize and Intuit.

Think of it as

- Relate to people
- Optimize resources
- Intuit—that is, access the wisdom inside yourself

The idea is to start with your Core Value and then refine your message.

See the next page for the Values-to-Message Progression Form

Values-to-Message Progression Form
(Authentic Leadership)

Example:

One of Your Personal Values	Innovation
Level of What #1 (What does that get you?)	Notice by investors and consumers
Level of What #2 (What does that get you?)	Market share
Level of What #3 (What does that get you?)	Financial success (or recognition)
Level of What #4 (What does that get you?)	Independence
Level of What #5 (What does that get you?)	Happiness *(This can be a personal benefit for the entrepreneur.)*
Attention Grabbing Authentic Message to Seize Team Members' Attention	"We innovate and we grab a big market share. We'll continue to make products that we want to make." *(Independence—a benefit noted on Level #4)*

© Tom Marcoux Media, LLC GetTheBigYES.com

Values-to-Message Progression Form
(Authentic Leadership)

One of Your Personal Values	
Level of What #1 (What does that get you?)	
Level of What #2 (What does that get you?)	
Level of What #3 (What does that get you?)	
Level of What #4 (What does that get you?)	
Level of What #5 (What does that get you?)	
Attention Grabbing Authentic Message to Seize Team Members' Attention	

© Tom Marcoux Media, LLC GetTheBigYES.com

I first introduced the *Relate Element* of RoiLeadership in a blog article. For a quick overview, here is a portion of that article from my blog GetTheBigYes.com:

How do you relate to yourself? Do you listen to your own feelings? Or do you stuff them down and ignore them?

Your ability to relate to others begins with your ability to know the truth in yourself and to be supportive of your own health and happiness. From a solid starting point, we then seek to effectively influence others.

"To create sustainable innovations ... connect with one another first, before trying to solve a problem."
– Michael J. Gelb

Psychiatrist and Professor Robert J. Waldinger of Harvard Medical School notes the results of an on-going 77 year-long study of happiness: **"The good life is built with good relationships."**

I'm going to briefly introduce elements of excellent leadership and relating. We often appreciate those leaders who are C.A.L.M. in the face of adversity.

C – call on intuition
A – agree
L – listen
M – measure

1. Call on intuition

Many top leaders mention how they use "gut feelings" to make critical decisions.

"Often you have to rely on intuition." – Bill Gates

"Intuition becomes increasingly valuable in the new information society precisely because there is so much data."
– John Naisbitt

"The only real valuable thing is intuition." - Albert Einstein

When it comes to relating well, we must pay close attention. When you listen to the person's vocal tone, the pacing of their speech, and their words, you're getting closer to understanding what they want. Add in observations of the body language and actions. The person might say, "I'm okay" – but your intuition may be warning you that something is going on beneath the surface communication.

Researcher and author Gerd Gigerenzer identifies intuition as connected with data that has not risen to the conscious level. He notes situations in which a person had a "bad feeling" but could not give a persuasive, rational argument. Then the company went ahead into what became a business disaster, and the person's "bad feeling" proved an accurate assessment.

Be sure to pay close attention to the other person, and make sure to listen to your own intuitive impressions.

2. Agree

"Agreements are courageous and creative. They honor the other person. They are coauthored between two composers of the agreement. People give their word and keep it. People honor agreements to a far greater degree than they live up to expectations." – Steve Chandler

Years ago, I learned that the leader does well to make sure that the team member makes a real commitment. I have asked, "Do you agree that you have all that you need to get the 1-2-3 Project done by 4 pm on Thursday?"

The person might come back with "Wait a minute. I can't agree to that because I won't get B part from Gerald in time."

This is vital information.

I've also learned to ask for further confirmation—because some people are too optimistic in their time projections.

Make sure you get the reply of "I agree…" from the other person.

3. Listen

Listening is the beginning of leadership. You need to know the person you're leading. He or she needs to know that they've been heard. (This is so important to me that I wrote a book, *Be Heard and Be Trusted*." I've emphasized with clients and graduate students: *When you're listening, you're winning.*

Many of us are quick to judge another person's comment—so fast it seems like a reflex. Learn to pause, take a breath, ask a gentle question and listen some more. Then, provide a *Reflective Reply*, which sounds like: "That sounds like it was disappointing." You reflect the person's feelings.

4. Measure

Team members count on the leader to demonstrate the team's current status. Are we making progress?

"People wouldn't go bowling if they couldn't see the pins drop." – Zig Ziglar

Make measurements as clear and simple as possible.

The team leader helps everyone get clear on what's necessary for vital progress.

Leaders also help the team members celebrate incremental progress.

This is crucial since much of what we do involves a "long haul."

* * *

In summary, when you want to improve your leadership skills (as a team leader—or even as a leader of your own life), focus on:

C – call on intuition
A – agree
L – listen
M – measure

In this reprint of one of my blog articles, I continue the discussion of values.

Blog article from GetTheBigYES.com

Secret for a Great New Year—Lead and Make a Big Difference

"What makes the difference so that I can make this year better than last year?" my client Alec asked.

"Leadership. Leading yourself and leading team members—even vendors or contractors," I replied.

I guide clients and audiences with my topic The RoiLeader. We're familiar with ROI as "return on investment." I add to this with *Relate, Optimize and Intuit.*

"Relate" is about excellent communication. When I give a speech or class on Authentic Leadership, I focus on the A.I.M. process:

A – adjust perspective
I – increase credibility
M – move through values

1. Adjust perspective

When someone follows a leader, the person has had a shift in perspective: "Oh, you're someone worth following."

When you start leading, you need to make sure that your team members shift to a perspective that creates a positive connection with you.

A powerful step is to demonstrate that you're truly listening. People want to be heard.

I have an elderly family member who does not listen to anyone. I don't trust him. My other family members also do not trust him.

Listening builds a foundation of trust.

My phrase is: *When you're listening, you're winning.*

Now it's your turn. When can you practice with a friend? Listen and then say something like: "What I heard you to say was _____. Do I have that about right?"

2. Increase credibility

When a new person encounters a leader, they have questions including:

- Can I trust you?
- Are you competent?
- Is your vision clear and can you lead us to good outcomes?
- Do you care about team members or do you use them like bathroom tissues?

We demonstrate our competence and strength of character with clear communication. We use headlines like: "I'll now share three possible ways to solve the XY problem …"

Next, we show that we're looking for input which can provide solutions better than our first guesses. We add something called a tagline*: "After I share three possible solutions, I'm going to open this up for discussion. I'm looking forward to hearing your thoughts and feelings about this. Together, we can come up with better ways to improve the situation."

Authors Lois P. Frankel and Carol Frohlinger share the ideas of headlines and taglines.

Now it's your turn. When will your practice boiling down your statement to clear headlines and taglines?

3. Move through values

When I say, "move through values," I mean that we move forward through the power of holding values. Not just profit and productivity—we're talking about "this is an environment where people grow."

Great leaders stand for a vision. Something like: "Yes! We can work well together and make something valuable for the customers. We'll fulfill their trust in us. We'll feel great as we fulfill our potential."

For example, the Imagineers for the Disney Parks hold to a vision. Tony Baxter (for decades a top Imagineer, creating sophisticated and delightful Disney Parks rides) wrote: "Guests still want to be astonished, and our best attractions deliver that wow factor with visions and emotions. I always start with the notion that it is the 20th repeat ride, not the first that is the most important."

Now it's your turn. What vision and values do you stand for? Make sure that you express these details in ways that reach your team members' hearts (where they live).

In summary, remember:

A – adjust perspective

I – increase credibility

M – move through values

These three focus areas form a key foundation for Authentic Leadership.

Yes, you can enhance Profits, Productivity and Potential.

We remember that team members excel when they have a supportive environment and meaningful work.

The RoiLeader shows the way. More than that, the RoiLeader lives the way.

Exercise 7:

Quickly, with no hesitation, write down eight values that mean something to you personally.

Now, circle your top four values.

To get the most from this book, write down your responses to the various exercises in a personal journal.

Jotting things down for even 20 seconds provides you with more value than merely reading.

Tom Marcoux

The RoiLeader Seizes
Opportunities to Lead

"I couldn't believe it. My manager said exactly the wrong thing that pissed off the whole team," my friend, Fred, said.

In my mind, I considered that his manager just had not received great training. And, repeatedly, Fred's manager *missed* opportunities to lead.

The RoiLeader does well to memorize the following questions so he or she does well in the heat of the moment.

I invite you to ask yourself the right questions so you *Seize Opportunities to Lead*

We'll use the 5 Questions of the L.E.A.D.S. process:

L – listening?

E – expressing fairness?

A – agreeing?

D – doing good—got a vision?

S – sharing headline and tagline?

1. Listening?
[Related to Relational Transparency]

"End this project," Jessica, a member of the board of directors said in the meeting.

"No!" I thought. I had made promises. I would see this project through to the end. This was a matter of honor.

But I could *not* deny the truth of what Jessica said.

This particular project had severe inherent problems with

its structure, how the marketplace would view it and the skill levels of those involved. I asked Jessica, "Is there anything else, you want me to know?"

"There is no way this project is going to make money," she said.

"I'm going to reflect on this. I'll have more thoughts on this. How about I give you a phone call this afternoon?" I replied.

"Sounds good," she said.

Upon reflection, I found that I agreed with Jessica's assessment. I canceled the project, and my company was able to grow into new, more profitable ventures.

Years later, I came across this quote:

"If it's not working, you can't polish a turd."
– Lee Unkrich, feature film director, creative team at Pixar

I've shared with clients and MBA students, my phrase "When you're listening, you're winning."

My points about that include:
- When you're listening, you're building trust in the relationship.
- When you're listening, you have the opportunity to hear new information and insights that can help you make better decisions.

2. Expressing fairness?
[Related to Balanced Processing]

When we're talking about fairness, I'm referring to giving opposing views a chance to be placed "on the table." I use the phrase: "Let's put that, like it's clay, on the table. We'll see what to keep and what to shave away."

I'm referring to a metaphor of using clay to create a great sculptured work of art.

RoiLeaders realize that an effective leader listens to all the information: the good and the bad ... the logical and the unusual. An unusual idea may serve as a springboard to better insights and action steps.

Over the years, I've seen often how team members respond with *more* innovative ideas when they know that it's safe to offer opposing views.

3. Agreeing?

[Related to Balanced Processing and Internalized Moral Perspective]

Years ago, the tension between me and "Allen," my then business partner, threatened to suffocate me.

He glared at me as we sat down to have a truce lunch in a restaurant.

My right leg fluttered like a hummingbird's wings. Fear coursed through my veins: I thought that the dissolution of the company would destroy the major project we were working on.

Still, in my heart, I knew that this company had to end.

We were at an impasse.

How could I possibly dissipate all the tension?

I got up to grab some napkins and to kindly pass a napkin to Allen.

But my suit jacket sleeve caught on my plastic cup of water.

Then—a surreal moment in which the plastic cup tilted on the verge of falling over ...

SPLASH! Water all over the table.

Allen and I both jumped to mop up the water with a stack

of napkins.

There was something we could agree on.

The moment with my suit jacket and the cup that splashed water was rather funny. And human.

With the tension dissipated, we moved forward and arrived at points of agreement.

Agreement is a prime process for the effective leader.

"Control leads to compliance; autonomy leads to engagement."
– Daniel H. Pink

The RoiLeader makes sure that the team member feels their autonomy and makes a true agreement to accomplish some task.

We return to one of my favorite quotes:

"Agreements are courageous and creative. They honor the other person. They are coauthored between two composers of the agreement. People give their word and keep it. People honor agreements to a far greater degree than they live up to expectations." – Steve Chandler

Agreements and Setting a System When Leading a Virtual Team

The RoiLeader gets the team member involved in setting up a system for high productivity and measuring progress.

At times, I'll have team members in the United States, United Kingdom and India simultaneously.

With each team member, I employ my experiences as a feature film director. Like an effective film director does *not* direct any two actors in the same manner, I customize how I interact with team members.

Working with editors, is something I do a lot. For example, this is my 45th book.

Working with an editor is an essential part of the book writing process.

On one book, I began with a new editor. Via email, I mentioned that I wanted to set a system so that my new editor, Lena, and I could efficiently work on hundreds of details that needed refinement.

As the leader, I might have tried to simply send her a list of "my requirements." That would have caused trouble because people often bristle at getting slammed with orders.

Instead, I called Lena, and we discussed a system of working together.

To assure that things would not get convoluted, I suggested that such a System might be 5 to 10 sentences.

Here are those sentences:

Tom and Lena System During Revision-Time
- Lena will add "LA" to the end of the document title to show that she has commented.
- Tom types "LQUESTION" in the document so Lena can do a "Search" and find and respond in the document.
- Lena will be ready to see on Monday, Wednesday, Friday an emailed version of the document so she can comment.
- Lena estimates that she can answer up to 5 questions likely in the same day. Over 5 questions likely takes the following day.

My point in sharing the above example is that Lena and I shaped this system, and we both agreed to it.

"We have three innate psychological needs—competence, autonomy, and relatedness. When those needs are satisfied, we're motivated, productive, and happy." – Daniel H. Pink

As you can see by my "Tom and Lena System," as a leader, I made sure that my editor felt the fulfillment of competence, autonomy and relatedness.

Exercise #8

As a leader, look for ways so your team members can experience autonomy. How can you invite your team member to come up with his/her own way of accomplishing the objective?

People will do what they agree to.

"Human beings have an innate inner drive to be autonomous, self-determined, and connected to one another. And when that drive is liberated, people achieve more and live richer lives."
– Daniel H. Pink

If a team member is simply ordered to do a task, then there is no opportunity to become engaged.

RoiLeaders know that engaged people create the extraordinary. So merely delivering orders is not good enough for RoiLeaders.

Sadly, with inadequate or no training in leadership, several managers will just default to telling people what to do.

Years ago, I led a team of young people. I had two entertainment franchises (graphic novels/movies/more) on the table. I asked each individual: "Which project would you prefer to work on—*TimePulse* or *Jack AngelSword*?" It was unanimous: all team members preferred to work on *Jack AngelSword*. Time and resources had already gone into *TimePulse*, a science fiction franchise of graphic novels and ultimately feature films.

However, upon receiving input from the team members, I discovered that I preferred working on *Jack AngelSword*, too. *Jack AngelSword* combined with *Jenalee Storm* (another character) has become the center of my company's entertainment division.

Earlier, I shared: people will do what they agree to. Certainly, in business, all team members find that they must do "grunt work" of some sort. We all have duties that can feel onerous. Still, if you can place team members into doing what they excel at and enjoy, you'll find that productivity and quality can soar upwards.

4. Doing good—got a vision?
The RoiLeader provides:
a) The vision
b) "the yardstick"
c) Meaningful, specific praise

Your team relies on you to have a vision and show the team a picture of an empowering future.
"Vision is the art of seeing what is invisible to others."
– Jonathan Swift

"Good business leaders create a vision, articulate the vision, passionately own the vision, and relentlessly drive it to completion." – Jack Welch

Team members want to know:
a) Where are we going?

b) Is it worthwhile to go there?

c) Does our leader have the competence to make the right decisions to get us there?

The RoiLeader demonstrates through well-chosen brief words the answers to the above questions.

The RoiLeader provides the "yardstick."

Think about it. How do we measure our progress? The RoiLeader *makes it a game you can win*. By this I mean, you pick reachable objectives.

In some instances—for example, a marketing campaign, we don't know if the marketplace will reward our efforts.

That's why it helps to separate goals into *Result-Goals* and *Effort-Goals.*

For example, the department needs 10 new clients. That's the Result-Goal. Each team member agrees to make 15 prospecting calls per day—that's the Effort-Goal.

The first week yields disappointing results.

So, the RoiLeader guides the team to refine their telephone conversation strategies.

The RoiLeader provides the "yardstick" and praises the team for good efforts.

Good praise is specific.

"The more you praise and celebrate your life, the more there is in life to celebrate." – Oprah Winfrey

"There are two things people want more than sex and money... recognition and praise." – Mary Kay Ash

"Nothing is more effective than sincere, accurate praise, and nothing is more lame than a cookie-cutter compliment."
– Bill Walsh

Good praise also points out the value. Here's an example: "I really appreciate how you ran through three scenarios and took action. That's saved us time and kept up our morale. Good work. Thank you for that."

Author and researcher, Carol S. Dweck points out that it's better to *not* praise people for "being talented." Why? If a person thinks they're talented, they may try to protect themselves from striving and taking a risk because they do *not* want to be proven "untalented."

Instead, praise the person for the intelligent effort that they put into the project. It takes effort to think something through. It takes persistent effort to get something done with quality.

"Why waste time proving over and over how great you are, when you could be getting better? Why hide deficiencies instead of overcoming them? Why look for friends or partners who will just shore up your self-esteem instead of ones who will also challenge you to grow? And why seek out the tried and true, instead of experiences that will stretch you? The passion for stretching yourself and sticking to it, even (or especially) when it's not going well, is the hallmark of the **growth mindset***. This is the mindset that allows people to thrive during some of the most challenging times in their lives." — Carol S. Dweck*

Refine your praise
Praise is supposed to be motivating.

"Outstanding leaders go out of their way to boost the self-esteem of their personnel. If people believe in themselves, it's amazing what they can accomplish." – Sam Walton

What's the opposite of good praise? The critical "Emotional Shutdown." For example, Steve Jobs was infamous for saying things like "That's the stupidest idea I ever heard."

Author Guy Kawasaki told me "I was one of the only people to survive working for Steve Jobs twice."

What happens when a supervisor says, "stupidest idea"? People shut down. Individuals decide: "I won't stick my neck out again."

When working on a project, it's easy to have certain perceptions. If a team member offers an idea that sounds unfeasible, I still pause and say, "I'm going to stir that in my soup for a while."

Again, when you seek to praise someone, be specific. Identify what actions led to good results.

Give Recognition; Give Ownership

RoiLeaders realize that engaged team members demonstrate heightened productivity and creativity.

"Find public ways to acknowledge others in the most sincere and meaningful ways…A brilliant example is the passing of the torch as a build-up to the Olympics. Every individual who carries it across the host country gains 'ownership' of the world-class event, and recognition for themselves, their organizations, and their communities." – Mark C. Thompson and Bonita S. Thompson

5. Sharing headline and tagline?

As leaders, we demonstrate our competence and strength of character with clear communication. We use headlines like: "I'll now share three possible ways to solve the XY problem …"

The RoiLeader uses a "headline" to concisely convey the point or objective he or she wants to put on the table.

Next, we show that we're looking for input which can provide solutions better than our first guesses. We add something called a "tagline": "After I share three possible solutions, I'm going to open this up for discussion. I'm looking forward to hearing your thoughts and feelings about this. Together, we can come up with better ways to improve the situation."

The RoiLeader develops *brief, compelling ways to communicate* so that the listener can take in the information. Even better, the listener is moved to participate or cooperate with what the RoiLeader is proposing.

Leadership is about helping your team know what they don't know, see what they can't see and ultimately, they feel empowered to do what they couldn't imagine doing.
– Tom Marcoux

As an Executive Coach, I move into times when I'm called on to take leadership—that is, I help the client see what they can't see in the moment.

In my work as an Executive Coach, I do *Solo Reflection Sessions.* During such a session, by myself, I reflect deeply on what I've heard the client say, I go over my notes and *think things through.* I also engage my intuition and feelings to access and observe what may be *hidden opportunities for my client.* During a Solo Reflection Session, I'm working on my client's business, and they're not even on the phone with me.

Later, I present my findings to the client. I also follow up with vital questions like:
- What did my comment bring up in you?
- Does that feel true?
- Is there something else that you want to add?

The above questions function like "taglines." These questions invite the client to think and feel in new directions.

Bonus Technique:
Encourage Them to Talk First

In high school, I felt a surge of energy when surrounded by other students, all asking me *what to do*, as I tackled my role as the director of a film. I always had a vision and an opinion.

Over decades of leading teams, I discovered something *different* and valuable: **Encourage your team member to talk first.**

When I get access to the intelligence, intuition and heartfelt focus of team members, my projects turn out to *exceed* my initial imaginings.

How do you get such access? You invite the other person to talk first.

I ask …
- "How are things going with the project?"
- "What's working?"
- "What are *Areas to Improve?*"
- "What do you need so you can do better with your part of the project?'
- "Is there something I need to know?"
- "Is there anything else I need to know?"

I have heard individuals ask, "Why do I always have to talk first? What do *you* think?"

Sometimes, I explain that "I don't want to colorize or influence the direction of the conversation."

My point here is that if you talk first, you might not hear the bad news or even innovative ideas. Why? People tend to, as social beings, talk in ways that they think will sound agreeable to the supervisor.

How to Internalize the Shift to Seize *Opportunities to Lead*

Exercise #9:

One of the exercises I've created for workshop participants includes handing out 3 X 5 cards to use in role-playing exercises.

Here are examples:

a) *Card Details:* "You talk first. You have to make your point first."
   (The Lost Opportunity to Lead is: _____)

b) *Card Details:* "You tell the person exactly how to do the task. You *avoid* asking for input."
   (The Lost Opportunity to Lead is: _____)

The RoiLeader and E-leadership

Related to Self-awareness, Relational Transparency, Balanced Processing and Internalized Moral Perspective

Some authors refer to E-leadership as "a social influence process, mediated by technology, to produce a change in attitudes, feelings, thinking, behavior, and performance with individuals, groups, or organizations to direct them toward achieving a specific goal."

When I think of E-leadership, I recall leading teams in India and the United Kingdom from my company workplace in the USA.

Most of my interactions were through chatting and email.

The RoiLeader must stay alert for the "landmines" that are present with those forms of communication.

Specific challenges arose when I worked with people with English as a second language.

Landmines in E-Leadership:
Bad timing and people feeling exhausted (physically and/or emotionally)

Here's an example. I was ending my day at about 1:30 AM. I saw someone I knew, George, online at Facebook.

(One of my errors was thinking that George knew me better than he did.)

I sent a chat-message to him: "I had a thought. You might want to use something like this."

I was leaving a link for a video that I had made.

George thought that I was selling something.

That was not my intention. Instead, I was attempting to do him a favor and share a marketing technique of using a certain form of video. My video would serve as an example that George could apply to his own marketing efforts.

As a fellow business owner and writer, I have empathy for George's work and life experience.

However, George cut off the conversation and attacked me with comments built on his assumption that I was ineptly trying to sell him something.

From this unfortunate and extreme misunderstanding, I learned some lessons that apply to improving one's E-Leadership skills.

Lessons

#1: Be careful about what time in your day you send a message.

#2: Be aware as to what time it is that the other person is receiving your message.

#3: Be careful that you do *not* think you have more of a bond with a colleague or "friend" than you do.

#4: When someone like a prospective client or business acquaintance goes on the attack, calm yourself and do *not* return negativity for negativity.

#5: Immediately use *Deescalating Language* to calm the situation down.

Toward the end of the interaction with George, I wrote in the Facebook chat:

"I learned something new.

I apologize for writing in too brief a manner.

—and not leading with questions.

So, thank you for devoting this time to our conversation.

I'm concerned that I kept you online too long.

Thank you for alerting me to my errors here.

Any other detail you want me to know?"

The above example reveals how chatting and email can lead to big misunderstandings and people even feeling offended.

The RoiLeader realizes that many people using email or chatting may be exhausted or *not* truly conscious of how close we can be to creating an unnecessary argument.

This section relates to Relational Transparency and Balanced Processing. That is, do *not* rely on the other person to be fully aware of the limitations and pitfalls of email, chatting, and similar tech-dependent ways of communicating.

About Deescalating Phrases
Here are examples of Deescalating Phrases:
- Thank you for alerting me to my errors here.
- Any other detail you want me to know?"

The power of Deescalating Phrases is that they show calm and respect. These are vital elements of true, Authentic Leadership.

Exercise #10:
Have you found yourself, at some time, in a big problem caused by some misunderstanding through email, a Facebook chat or text? What did you do to resolve the situation? How could you have avoided the whole misunderstanding? How could you have used *Deescalating Phrases?*

With E-leadership, Take Full Advantage of Your Tech Tools

Use images and videos to quickly communicate your points:

For example, when I hire a new vendor, I tell this story. Decades ago, I hired a printer to print some books. I said that I had a small budget. The printer took that comment to heart and did *not* tell me about putting varnish on the cover of 500 books. The price to add varnish? $100.00

He printed the books which proved unusable because the ink came off the book cover onto the reader's hands.

If he had told me about the additional $100.00 expense, I would have found a way to pay for it.

In terms of E-leadership, I could have a short video made that illustrates the story about the ink running onto readers' hands. Then, I could have my assistant provide that video for any new vendors. I would save time because I would avoid having to tell the same story multiple times.

I could address the video camera and say: "Thank you for applying to be a vendor for my company. The moral of my story is that I want to know the details—like that $100.00 for the book cover—so I can make the best decision. Thank you."

PART THREE
Optimize

Related to Self-awareness, Relational Transparency, Balanced Processing and Internalized Moral Perspective

Here, we'll discuss *Optimize*, the "O" portion of the R.O.I. Leader process.

As leaders, we're called to guide team members to great purpose and productivity.

In this section, we'll Lead like a P.R.O.:

P – Protect the Talent

R – Reward Momentum

O – Optimize for Excellence and Expansion

1.   Protect the talent

As a feature film director, I have needed to get the best performances from actors and crew people. I learned that two principles are valuable: Protect the Talent and Guard Momentum. (I'll talk about momentum in the next section.)

On a feature film set, "the talent" refers to the male and female actors (this distinction is emphasized by the Screen Actors Guild).

Your team members are the Talent. In fact, you are the talent, too.

On the set (for example a sunny beach), I made sure that people got what they needed to do their jobs well. On the set we focus on getting people out of the sun, using umbrellas, providing water and meals.

What can you do to make sure your team members (and you, too!) have what you need to do well? Remember … Protect the Talent.

2. Reward momentum

I directed my first short film when I was nine years old. My first cameraman was my father. I learned quickly that no one moves unless the leader provides direction. To get the material filmed on a particular afternoon, I had to Guard Momentum.

As a student filmmaker, I'd pick up that camera (when necessary) and say, "Okay. Everyone, we're going over there." My pacing guided the pacing for the group.

How do you "reward momentum"? You praise people for guarding momentum. You tell people that you're guarding your own momentum. You set up structures, so team members guard each other's momentum.

You invite team members to say something like "Are you on a roll? How about you send me a text message when you're available?"

You provide actual rewards for people who move forward. Even taking a team member for a celebratory "You moved forward on XY Project" cup of coffee is "rewarding momentum."

Make momentum a value that the team members uphold right next to Guard Quality.

(By the way "Guard Quality" relates to the next section: Optimize for Excellence and Expansion.)

3. Optimize for Excellence and Expansion

Many of us realize to optimize something, we'll need to make excellent choices.

About Excellence

Set Criteria for Excellence—that is, identify what is crucial so that your project works well for the customers/end users. Identify the Critical Elements for excellent performance. Additionally, identify what you can drop.

There are times when perfectionists get in trouble. A supervisor may comment about a perfectionist's efforts: "That's nice. But that's not what we really need."

To avoid such an error, use these questions:

• What must be in this project?

• What can we drop? (I refer to "droppables")

• What do the stakeholders (customers/others) most want in this project?

• What do customers/end users most need from this project?

• What is most important to our team/company/humankind* about this project?

Some might ask, "Humankind?" And I reply: "Why not strive to make a contribution to the human enterprise?"

Here is another facet of striving for and achieving excellence. You need to provide evaluation for yourself and others.

I've introduced clients to "The Evaluation Box."

You identify your Top Three Focus Areas (and place them in the "Evaluation Box").

Andrea, one of my clients, uses these three Focus Areas: Health, Increase Income and Destiny-Work. Each week, she reviews her efforts. She assigns a color:

• Green – Good

• Yellow – Concerned

• Red – in Trouble; Fix This

Meanwhile, Sarah has three people who directly report to her. In a weekly meeting, she has team members identify their current status with their projects. They simply and clearly state the status of the projects with Green, Yellow or Red.

What are your Top Three Focus Areas? How will you evaluate your progress?

* * *

In summary, part of being a good leader (at work and in your own life) involves seeing things clearly.

Remember:

P – Protect the Talent

R – Reward Momentum

O – Optimize for Excellence and Expansion

Exercise #11:

How can you protect the talent? Can you make sure there are adequate breaks and that the schedule provides for adequate recovery time? How will you reward momentum? How will you encourage team members to guard momentum?

Additional Notes on …

Optimize Excellence and Expansion

The Imagineers for the Disney Parks hold to a vision. Tony Baxter (for decades a top Imagineer, creating sophisticated and delightful Disney Parks rides) wrote: "Guests still want to be astonished, and our best attractions deliver that wow factor with visions and emotions. I always start with the notion that it is the 20th repeat ride, not the first that is the most important."*

I mentioned this quote earlier. It bears repeating here because it's an example of expanding one's thinking.

Expand Your Thinking with Good, Excellent, Amazing!
To lead well, we need to think on an expansive level.

Every week, when working with my own coach, I identify my weekly goals on Three Levels: Good, Excellent and Amazing!

• Good – I know these tasks are vital and I can complete them
• Excellent – These tasks require that I stretch
• Amazing! – These tasks require alliances and expansive thinking.

With Cynthia, a client, I helped her identify her own goals for a particular week:
• Good – work on revising my business's website
• Excellent – make 19 marketing phone calls
• Amazing! – complete all revisions of my website after having 11 people give me feedback.

Optimize Excellence: Speak with Brevity and High-Level Competence
Rehearse what you will say in a meeting *before the meeting.* Keep your comments brief, on point and valuable.

"Time is the new money." – Richard Branson

Exercise #12:

Will you use the Good-Excellent-Amazing! Pattern of setting goals in your own life? Who can be your Accountability Partner (someone to whom you mention your progress each week)?

The RoiLeader and "Optimize" #2

Lead and Handle Complexity

"How do we manage the complexity?" – Bernard T. Ferrari

"It's too complicated and I feel confused. I just want some clarity," my client, Matthew, said.

"I hear you. We've talked about your packed To-Do List. I've learned that a To-Do list is often a Guilt-List," I replied.

It's valuable to pull out the most important tasks from your complicated and crowded To-Do List.

When you do this, **you get clarity, and you guard your personal energy. Bonus!—You banish feeling overwhelmed.**

We'll use the F.O.C.U.S. process:

F – Find options
O – organize by *the most important*
C – count on three
U – uncover your results
S – strategize for "droppables"

1. Find options
(Tool: Consider Box)

What's most important for you to do today—or this week?

So many ideas are vague, and you'll ultimately discard them. You don't want them cluttering your To-Do List.

Place them in the Consider Box.

With my own coach, I mention some ideas for future

projects and future marketing plans. I note them and put them aside "into the Consider Box."

It's important to guard your personal energy. When an idea/task is in the Consider Box, it is not active, and you *avoid feeling guilty* about not getting around to it.

What do you want to put into your Consider Box?

2. Organize by *the most important*
(Tool: Progress One Page)

Something is the most important for you. Use one page to track your progress. Some of my clients track their daily exercise on one page (taped to their bathroom mirror).

Jerry Seinfeld gave a young comic, Brad Isaac, a tool that has become known as "Jerry Seinfeld's Productivity Secret."

Jerry said: "Put a big wall calendar for a year on a wall. For every day, you do your writing, you get to put a big red X over that day. After a few days you'll have a chain. Just keep at it, and the chain will grow longer every day. You'll like seeing that chain, especially when you get a few weeks under your belt. Your only job next is to not break the chain. Don't break the chain."

Using the Progress One Page follows the pattern that Jerry talked about.

3. Count on three
(Tool: Top 3 Sheet)

For example, at one point, I held certain priorities:
- Revise my novel
- Write a webinar
- Revise my leadership book

With my *Top 3 Sheet*, I made sure to do these tasks every day and check them off.

The Top 3 Sheet is one page in which you list your top

three most important tasks, and you check them off daily. Some of my clients keep their Top 3 Sheet on corkboard where they can see it daily.

I have a phrase: **Make it a game you can win.**

4. Uncover your results

(Tool: Evaluation Box)

One of my clients identified three top priorities for the week: health, efforts that bring in clients and long-term enjoyable work.

Every week, we went over her list. She would apply an evaluation of her weekly progress per her three top priorities:

Green – good
Yellow – caution
Red – it's a problem; fix this.

The power of this Evaluation Box system is that you're holding yourself accountable. You stay aware of what you're doing and what you're failing to do.

You'll find that using this pattern of "awareness leading to correction" to be helpful.

5. Strategize for "droppables"

(Tool: Select Droppables)

"The essence of strategy is choosing what not to do."
– Michael Porter

"Deciding what not to do is as important as deciding what to do." — Steve Jobs

We can't do it all. Not at one point in time. And some tasks/projects become obsolete. At one point, I had two major projects *TimePulse* and *Jack AngelSword*. These are entertainment franchises that will feature books/screenplays/graphic novels/toys and more.

My intuition gave me a question to ask new interns working with my company: Which would you rather work on *TimePulse* or *Jack AngelSword?* Unanimously, the new interns said, "Jack AngelSword."

My entertainment franchise work is for young people and others. On hearing such feedback, I realized that *I* preferred to work on *Jack AngelSword*, too. (This year, I'm releasing two novels of the *Jenalee Storm* series, featuring *Jack AngelSword*.)

So, I completed a book (a collection of my short fiction) that had three *TimePulse* stories in it. And then, I made *TimePulse* a droppable. That is, I dropped *TimePulse* from my company's schedule.

At another time, I had 14 projects on my corkboard. I dropped six and quickly completed four projects. Then, I carried onward with four. *If you feel overwhelmed, see what you can make into a "droppable."*

In summary, **be sure to focus on the most important.**

The Tools I shared are:

- Consider Box
- Progress One Page
- Top 3 Sheet
- Evaluation Box
- Select Droppables

Exercise #13:

Which of the Tools will you experiment with? What real, upcoming accomplishments mean the most to you? How will you use a Tool(s) to move forward with greater consistency?

PART FOUR
Intuit

> *Related to Self-awareness, Relational Transparency, Balanced Processing and Internalized Moral Perspective*

"Is it time to stop this product line?" my client, Anna, asked me.

"What are your thoughts and feelings about this?" I asked, serving as her Spoken Word Strategist and Executive Coach.

"Part of me thinks I should stay with what I know, and part of me thinks that the market has moved on," she said.

"Instead of setting up two opponents—this part of you and that rigid part of you … Let's just say that you're having some thoughts in one direction and some thoughts in the other direction," I replied. "So, what do you feel about this product line? Don't hesitate."

"It must end," Anna said. "That was the phrase that just rose up in my mind."

"Let's look at that," I replied.

"Don't let the noise of others' opinions drown out your own inner voice. And most important, have the courage to follow your heart and intuition." – Steve Jobs

"It is always with excitement that I wake up in the morning wondering what my intuition will toss up to me, like gifts from the

sea. I work with it and rely on it. It's my partner." – Jonas Salk

"Intuition will tell the thinking mind where to look next."
– Jonas Salk

As I address MBA students and audiences, I'm often asked, "How do you tell which 'inner voice' you're hearing?"

In the course of providing an answering, I note this difference:

- *The Voice of Fear* says, "Contract, hide, do not take risks."
- *The Voice of Intuition* says, "Expand, experiment, take an appropriate risk."

How do you get access to intuition? Do appropriate experiments. What's appropriate?

You can identify important questions for yourself like:

- Can you try a marketing campaign that will *not* break your budget?
- Can you trying a marketing message that will *not* hurt your credibility?

Intuition and the A.C.T.I.O.N. Process

Sometimes, my clients ask, "Where do I apply my intuition?" In response, I devised the A.C.T.I.O.N. process:

A - arrange a "Say YES to Myself" project
C - consider "Venues where Coordinators Say YES to Me'
T - target a "Tipping Point Form of Marketing"
I - identify "10 Friends" (Amazing Happens With Alliances)

O - organize better Enrollment Call Closes (rehearsals)
N - nurture "Designated Days"

1. Arrange a "Say YES to Myself" project

This form of project is one that you can launch yourself. You do *not* need anyone's permission. For example, one can write a book, hire an editor and publish the book through Amazon's departments including Kindle and their print-on-demand service.

It's reported that Sigmund Freud's first book and Deepak Chopra's first book were self-published. They took action and did not wait for some publisher to give them a nod of approval and "yes."

2. Consider "Venues where Coordinators Say YES to Me"

Authors and speakers find that they want to speak at major conferences. This process requires a meeting planner/committee to say "yes" to you.

Numerous Event Coordinators Ask about:
- Total Number of Fans or Clients on One's Email List
- Total Number of Facebook Likes and Friends
- Total Number of Twitter Followers
- Total Number of YouTube Subscribers

3. Target a *Tipping Point Form of Marketing*

One example of a Tipping Point Form of Marketing is the hybrid of podcast (on iTunes) and YouTube show recorded simultaneously. I call this a *Tipping Point Form of Marketing* because there is "no ceiling." You can get an extraordinary number of YouTube subscribers and iTunes listeners.

4. Identify "10 Friends" (Amazing Happens With Alliances)

The idea of "10 Friends" is to gather a group of business owners who choose to cross-promote each other's products. This pattern is often used by authors and creators of online courses.

5. Organize better Enrollment Call Closes (rehearsals)

You can use your intuition and your observations to conduct better Enrollment Calls. In my book, *Relax, You Don't Need to Sell*, I discuss a process that is better than traditional sales, known as "enrollment." In an enrollment call, you learn what the prospective client's wants to happen and what they consider as current obstacles.

A difficulty for several people is to "close the sale" or "gain the client." Here's where intuition can help. You might get the intuitive impression that people hesitate to hire you because they do *not* truly believe that you can solve their problem.

This is important information. Now, you can rehearse with someone you trust and practice clear ways to ask appropriate questions. In this manner, you build your skills, so you more readily gain a prospective clients trust.

6. Nurture "Designated Days"

Having Designated Days is a time management tool. The idea is to select a particular day of the week to focus your energy on a specific project.

Examples of Designated Days:
a) Enrollment Calls
b) My book
c) My revised website.

Exercise #14:

Write on a sheet of paper, the A.C.T.I.O.N. topics.
Then write 3 options for each topic:

A - arrange a "Say YES to Myself" project
C - consider "Venues where Coordinators Say YES to Me"
T - target a "Tipping Point Form of Marketing"
I - identify "10 Friends" (Amazing Happens With
   Alliances)
O - organize better Enrollment Call Closes (rehearsals)
N - nurture "Designated Days"

Circle the options that feel like the best fit at this moment.
Now, you have an Action Plan.

We explore how to M.O.V.E. on your intuition:

To gain the advantage of using your intuition for your
best performance in a speech or pitch, you need to move—
that is, take action.

1. Make space for your intuition

What do you use as the opening of your pitch? You can
make space for your intuition by saying, "I'll just see how it
feels over the next couple of days." This is an "open"
approach as opposed to shutting down your process quickly.

Unfortunately, many individuals have not practiced being
okay for a duration of uncertainty. Top innovators know
that you need to tinker with a problem for a time—to come
up with an excellent solution

Be sure to try your opening line of your pitch with several
people. Notice how you feel as you say the line. Give it time

(and space) for you to discover what works well.

2. Observe closely and "listen" to your intuition

At one point, I was preparing a speech, and I invited 11 people to hear various versions of the speech. They all had varying opinions.

Over the years, I've realized that one does *not* have to take in or use every different opinion.

It's not just what other people say, it is what *you* feel as you do the speech or pitch.

As you practice saying your ideas out loud, you get experiences, so you can sense what feels like a true fit for you.

3. Validate your intuition

Keep a log of times your intuition was correct, and you improved your life by acting based on your intuitive impression. When you have a written log, you have evidence that your intuition serves you well.

4. Energize through rehearsal

Top actor Kenneth Branagh said, "I used to call it fear [stage fright], but now I call it excitement because it is more useful."

As the Spoken Word Strategist and Executive Coach, I guide clients to devote even just 9 minutes a day to rehearsal (preferably early in the day) so they can get their subconscious mind involved in their process. When you work for 9 minutes in the morning, your subconscious mind works on your speech at various times during your whole day.

* * *

In summary, make space for your intuition to help you.

When your intuition is well-developed, you can even modify details spontaneously—during your pitch—to connect well with your current audience of investors.

Remember:

M – Make space for your intuition

O – Observe closely and "listen" to your intuition

V – Validate your intuition

E – Energize through rehearsal

Exercise #15:

When can you schedule brief rehearsals? You could take two minutes to rehearse the opening of a speech or something you'll present to the Board of Directors (for example).

Additional Notes on:

Make space for your intuition

"If you don't have time to do it right, when will you have time to do it over?" - John Wooden

"Are you telling me, you cannot wait 24 hours to think this through? And to feel your way through this?" I asked Steven, a client.

"No. I guess I *could* sleep on it. And see how I feel about this decision in the morning," he said.

"Exactly!" I replied.

Observe closely and "listen" to your intuition

"What do you know to be true?" I asked my client,

Karina.

"I don't know enough."

"I get that," I said. "Pause. Take in a breath. Good. What do you know to be true?"

"I'm feeling overwhelmed. I'm being pulled to do the three projects."

"When a client tells me 'I'm overwhelmed,' I listen to that. *And* when a client tells me *I'm being pulled to do something,* I listen to that, too," I said. "Let's keep talking. We can discover a Third Alternative."

"What's that?" she asked.

"Years ago, author Stephen R. Covey wrote about two people sharing an office. One wanted the window closed. The other wanted the window open. The idea was to keep talking. Why did one person want the window closed? The breeze caused his papers to flutter. They kept talking until the *third alternative* was found—open a window in the adjoining office."

"You mean I could do both?—reduce my feeling overwhelmed and still carry on with the projects?"

I smiled. "Yes. It's possible. How would you do that?"

Karina took in a big breath. "I guess I could just do one project and postpone the other two to next month or after that."

"Sounds like a good start," I replied.

Exercise #16:

Keep a journal. When you get an intuitive impression, write it down. See how things turn out. Write down the outcome of your taking action based on your intuitive impression.

PART FIVE:
RoiLeaders Hone Their Communication Skills

> *Related to Self-awareness, Relational Transparency, Balanced Processing and Internalized Moral Perspective*

RoiLeaders Hone Their Communication Skills #1

The Hidden Secret RoiLeaders Use to Communicate and Truly Influence People

"What lesson did you learn that was expensive, that you had to pay for, but it's made your life better?" my friend, Mark, asked me.

"*Do everything you can to be an exceptional listener.* I had the greatest teacher who did the opposite—who did not listen and created catastrophes."

"Who is that?"

"My father. He gave me a backhanded gift. I wanted to be *unlike* him. To this day, family members do *not* trust him—because he does *not* listen, he does *not* admit his errors, and he does *not* get better," I said, from my heart.

To become an Exceptional Listener, we use the N.O.W. process:

N – nurture your listening skills
O – open your mind to your internal obstacles
W – wrestle and rise above your previous limits

1. Nurture your listening skills

"You cannot heal what you do not acknowledge, and what you do not consciously acknowledge will remain in control of you from within, festering and destroying you and those around you."
– Richard Rohr

Why do you press on, keep talking, and, at times, fail to listen?

Here are some details that have been voiced by my students and clients:

- Listening takes time. I'm afraid that we don't have the time.
- Some people really don't get it. I don't want my team to be swayed by stupid ideas.
- I don't want the meeting to descend into a complaint-fest—people just complaining.

I've learned that the leader sets the tone.

For example, with my MBA students, I have asked, "What is working for you? And, what do you want more of?" at the end of the initial class.

You'll notice that *I have set the tone as positive.*

Because I often work with an international group of students, I have them write down their answers anonymously. Some cultures hold that if you speak up and ask questions, you might be disrespectful to the instructor.

So, I provide the quiet students with a way of "talking to me" through their anonymous responses on slips of paper that they hand in.

Then, in the next class, I read the comments and I respond to the comments in real time with the students.

They also see how I might add something to the session

because I am listening to their comments, and I'm incorporating their preferences when appropriate.

2. Open your mind to your internal obstacles
Listening is hard work. That's the truth.

We need to observe our internal obstacles. What about our current fears and internal pain keeps us from devoting our full attention?

Several years ago, I found myself making a big mistake while directing my first feature film. I was so enthusiastic and grateful to be directing the film that I *gushed* my thank-yous and appreciation.

I watched faces. I was coming across as "too much." The actors and crew faces communicated: "Is this guy for real?"

Upon reflection, I imagined that some of my frantic energy included "if they don't like me, they won't do what I say."

Here are examples of "internal obstacles":
- "Trying to hard" because you're afraid of something.
- Feeling overwhelmed so you have too little energy to devote to each person and each conversation.

You need to take great care of yourself, so you have a big reservoir of personal energy.

What do you need that energy for? To **communicate to people in the way that they prefer to receive the messages—and in a way they CAN receive the messages.**

As a feature film director, I learned to direct each actor in a unique way, customized to the person in front of me.

3. Wrestle and rise above your previous limits
I've said, "I was so focused on the deadline that I didn't hear you out last time. Continue. I'm listening carefully."

I've learned from my interactions with my father that one can't trust someone who does not admit errors. Why? Someone who refuses to see his or her own humanness cannot change for the better.

To rise above your past errors, ask a family member or team member: "What works for you when we have a conversation?" and "What gets in the way when we're talking?"

You might hear something like:
- I really need you to boil it down to your main point. You give me too much detail and then I don't know what's really important.
- You talk too quickly. And you assume that I have details that I don't have. Maybe you could ask me if I've heard about something, so we know we're on the same page.
- Just tell me what you want. You have this way of asking a question instead of just coming out and telling me what you need.

In summary, to lead other people, listening well is an essential tool. It involves getting internal obstacles out of the way and asking appropriate questions including:
- What's most important to you about …?
- What works for you when we have a conversation?
- What gets in the way when we're talking?
- What is working for you? And what do you want more of?

Rehearse with a friend or trusted colleague so you improve your conversation skills.

Additional Notes on …

The RoiLeader Thinks a Topic Through and Boils the Point to Few Words

Above, we noted Core Values.

One vital Core Value for the RoiLeader is: **Provide clear, vivid, and brief communication.**

In today's marketplace, we're all moving at a dizzying pace.

Many people say or at least think: "Got it. What's next?"

For example, the RoiLeader develops themes or phrases that stick.

Several years ago, I worked as part of the team that accomplished placing Wells Fargo as the first bank using Online Banking.

The leader of the group said, "Fail forward fast."

The software and logistics had never been done before.

Our team knew that we were going to develop software that was "going to break," and we'd fix the bugs fast.

"Fail forward fast" was easy to remember, and we took it to heart.

Here are some examples of phrases I use to convey ideas in a brief, catchy manner:
- Make it a game you can win.
- Lead So I Follow, Speak So I Believe.
- Keep Score and Achieve More.
- Motion Brings Clarity.

To Get to Memorable Statements of Core Values, the RoiLeader Thinks It Through and Feels It, Too

What can be a company's Core Values?

Here's an example: Disneyland

Earlier, I shared this example:

In 1965, Van France, at Disneyland, created a set of standards that would help *Cast Members* (Disney's term for their employees) create happiness for *Guests* (Disney's term for customers).

Van France identified:

- Safety
- Courtesy
- Show
- Capacity (later identified as "Efficiency")

Let's get specific. Related to "Show," Cast Members devote efforts to maintain the illusion of a particular land. You do *not* see a Cast Member in an astronaut's suit walk through Frontierland.

How about "Efficiency"? In recent years, Disney has innovated the Fast Pass which is a system that gives the Guests a specific time to arrive at an attraction. This system cuts down on crowding and wait times. That certainly increases the Guests' happiness.

Pause Now: What are your Core Values?

In today's world, we don't have time for long "mission statements."

I prefer what I call a "Mission Caption" that people can memorize. And if you're the CEO, memorize it.

My company's mission caption is: *We create energizing, encouraging edutainment for our good and humankind's rise.*

My personal mission statement is: *I help people experience enthusiasm, love and wisdom to fulfill Big Dreams.*

As the Spoken Word Strategist, I'm focused on *Words and Performance that Inspire Feelings.*

Since I picked up my first movie camera at age 9, my focus continues as *pulling the best performance out* of actors or the crew members.

As an Executive Coach, I help my client pull out their best performances, too.

My point in sharing the above details is: As a RoiLeader, you need to refine your language. Make your words brief and powerful.

A couple of hours ago, I said to a client, "Remember: Less Words—Better Words."

"The only limit to your impact is your imagination and commitment." – Tony Robbins

As an RoiLeader, consider these values:
- Courage
- Self-discipline
- Get material into the marketplace.

These values are crucial because you will get criticism tossed at you. I came up with a ritual when criticism shows up. I call it "Celebrate Someone Disagrees." People can only disagree when you have your material (your products) out in the marketplace.

I'm really celebrating how my team and I demonstrate our courage, self-discipline and dedication to get material into the marketplace.

Exercise #17:

What is a vital Core Value to you?

In your personal journal, write down a first draft of your expressing that material.

You'll notice that your first draft likely has a lot of words.

See if you can delete some of the words and make the statement have more impact.

Example:

When I was young, I directed films and I pulled good performances out of actors. (15 words)

Revision:

As a film director, I inspire actors' best performances. (8 words)

RoiLeaders Hone Their Communication Skills #2

Use Effective Body Language in Your Pitch or Speech—Get Funding

From my blog PitchPowerFest.com

"You're saying that the wrong body language can destroy my chance to pitch and get funding?" my client, Matthew asked.

"The wrong body language can affect the investors on the subconscious level. They won't believe you have the confidence to be successful. That means that they'll fund someone else's project," I said.

Learn Two Critical Elements of Body Language

1. Do NOT Dismiss an Investor who seems to have "Closed Body Language"

If you step into a bookstore, you can find books on body language that proclaim that if a person has her arms crossed, she might be "closed off" to your idea.

Maybe.

She could also be cold. Or she simply finds that crossing her arms feels comfortable to her.

Here's the point: The folded arms provide you with only one data point.

Some researchers refer to a form of "resting face" that unintentionally appears as if a person is irritated, contemptuous, angry, or simply annoyed. This expression is known as RBF — "Resting B__ch Face."

I've seen some audience members (with folded arms and frowns) come up after a speech then break into a smile and tell me: "Tom, I really like the ideas you shared with us! The material is so useful."

So be careful. Do *not* stop talking to people who look "closed off." Address the whole audience because you want every chance to connect with potential investors.

2. Make Your Body Language Congruent with What You Say

If you say, "I'm confident that my product can solve your situation," while you're wringing your hands, what will the investors believe—your words or your hands?

Your hands will be "too loud" and their actions will "drown out" your words.

Here's another vital point: Do *not* take a step backwards when hit with a tough question.

Taking a step backwards makes you look scared and lacking in confidence. When I share this in workshops, several audience members nod their heads. That's fine.

Then I raise the conversation up to a better place. I say: *"Explanation does NOT equal transformation. ... We're now going to practice walking toward the person who asks a question."*

[In my workshops, people address a small audience of two—because the audience is divided into "Teams of Three."]

The truth is you need to practice and rehearse effective body language.

Additionally, in my work as the Spoken Word Strategist and Executive Coach, I have my private clients practice taking one or two steps forward toward the person who asked the question. Just one or two steps forward—and not too close. The Effective Body Language says, "I'm devoting my full attention to you. I am not intimidated by your question. I am confident."

In summary, pay close attention to the vital elements of body language.

With good, strong body language, you can be winning during a pitch even before you open your mouth. Additionally, make sure to keep the investors' perception of you as confident by taking a couple of steps toward a person who asks you a question.

Remember, body language can drown out your words. Keep your words and body language congruent.

Exercise #18:

Ask a trusted friend to watch you deliver part of a speech. What "ticks" or subconscious body motions do you do? Which motions make you look like you lack confidence? How can you transform that?

(Example: Some people rubs their hands in a nervous way. Solution: Make gestures and keep your hands away from each other.)

Tom Marcoux

PART SIX:
RoiLeaders Make Great Decisions While Facing Risk

Related to Self-awareness, Relational Transparency, Balanced Processing and Internalized Moral Perspective

Roi Leaders Make Great Decisions While Facing Risk #1

Take the Right Risk

"Challenge is the crucible for greatness. Every single personal-best leadership case involved change from the status quo. ... Regardless of the specifics, they all involved overcoming adversity and embracing opportunities to grow, innovate, and improve. Leaders are pioneers willing to step into the unknown."
– James M. Kouzes and Barry Z. Posner

Where does big prosperity come from? Learn how to make excellent choices and take the Right Risks. This is a source of Real Power.

Some people know that Walt Disney's first company Laugh-O-Gram Studio went bankrupt. It must have hurt an extra amount because Walt had seen his father fail at several business ventures, too.

Disneyland was a huge risk. More than that, everyone was against it: Walt's wife Lillian, his brother/business partner Roy O. Disney and the board of directors. Walt cashed in his life insurance to pay for the first designs of Disneyland.

These details inspired me to think about how we might choose well when a risky choice arises.

My intuition gave me certain questions to help me ascertain if something is what I call the "Right Risk."

- Will I grow?
- Will I learn?
- Will I make new alliances?
- Can I avoid "losing the store"?
- Can I make money all the while?
- Does my heartfelt intuition call me to go forth in this direction?

Now, I'll talk a bit about each question and add some wise council from Walt Disney.

• Will I grow? Will I learn?

I've written over 2 million words. Over the years, I have been working to improve in the craft of writing—both nonfiction and fiction. I don't get stuck like I did several years ago. I've learned how to jump in and get writing even when I don't feel like. Writing has become like dancing to me: You stretch, you learn the steps and then you have moments of real grace.

Many of us writers learn to revise and revise.

"Get a good idea and stay with it. Dog it, and work at it until it's done right." – Walt Disney

• Will I make new alliances?

Many times, we make the biggest strides forward when we team up or at least get some coaching. This is one of the reasons why I find so much meaning as the Spoken Word Strategist and Executive Coach. I help my clients learn things faster, get unstuck and streamline their process to reach higher levels of success and fulfillment.

My phrase is: **Alliances make advances.**

I've hired more than ten editors. I've learned from each one. Often, we go farther faster when we team up with effective people.

For example: In the early years, Ub Iwerks drew Mickey Mouse for the first animated Disney films. Without Ub's contribution, Mickey would not have looked nor moved the way he did. This is an example of the power of alliances: Walt Disney's story sense and Ub's design/animation sense.

Later, Ub left the Disney Company to head his own studio. This bothered Walt a lot. Still, it's said that of all the telegrams that arrived to celebrate the success of Snow White and the Seven Dwarfs, Walt kept only one telegram—the one from Ub.

Years later, Ub returned to call upon Walt. Ub wanted a job, and Walt gave him the facilities so Ub could experiment with some technical processes. One of Ub's advances made it possible to efficiently make the feature film, *101 Dalmatians.*

Walt had a habit: He would ask the team members to "plus" [add to/improve] each scene of a film.

Now it's your turn.

How can you team up with effective people?

What gaps in your knowledge or resources do you need shored up by working with others?

Write down notes about how you can gain team members or collaborate with others.

• **Can I avoid "losing the store"?**
"Everyone falls down. Getting back up is how you learn how to

walk." – Walt Disney

My point is: Build in a buffer zone so you avoid "losing the store." By this I mean, be careful about a budget and the use of resources. If possible, avoid spending too much on a project.

Some people note that in the same year James Cameron spent $200 million on *Titanic*, Steven Spielberg spent $63 million on *Jurassic Park*.

We realize that *Titanic* called for more expenditures. They built a replica of the great ship, for example.

Still, Steven Spielberg is a master of choosing what to place in a movie and what to leave out.

For example, a river scene with attacking pterodactyls was dropped from *Jurassic Park* (considered too expensive) and only revived for *Jurassic Park III*.

"The difference in winning and losing is most often... not quitting." – Walt Disney

To avoid quitting, it can be helpful to retain some money to keep going.

Be careful of budgets of time, money and other resources.

• Can I make money all the while?

When the Walt Disney Company opens a new theme park they start with a few rides. Then over the years they add more attractions.

"Disneyland is like a piece of clay: If there is something I don't like, I'm not stuck with it. I can reshape and revamp."
– Walt Disney

At the Disneyland Resort, when California Adventure Park opened several things didn't go as planned. In the first year 2001, only 5 million visitors attended. To give perspective to that, in that same year Disneyland saw 12.3 million visitors. In response, the Disney team lowered ticket prices.

How bad were things? The park only had about 5,000 to 9,000 visitors on weekdays although it was built to have a capacity of 33,000.

Okay. That was a rocky start. Disney CEO Bob Iger announced a multi-year revision of the park. It had cost $600 million to build California Adventure Park. The Disney team would further invest $1.1 billion to revise and remodel the park. Let's remember the idea "make money all the while." California Adventure has been open and earning income across the years.

One detail that captures my interest is that the entrance area was changed to a representation of Los Angeles as it appeared when Walt Disney moved there in the 1920s. What a great idea! This brings in the element of magical, nostalgia energy similar to Disneyland's Main Street U.S.A.

Find ways to bring something to the marketplace and keep improving the product in subsequent versions.

• Does my heartfelt intuition call me to go forth in this direction?

"When you're curious, you find lots of interesting things to do. And one thing it takes to accomplish something is courage."
– Walt Disney

A number of people have asked me, "How did you write 45 books, Tom?"

I reply, "I was called to each one. I wanted to go on the journey of writing each particular book."

"You reach a point where you don't work for money."
– Walt Disney

Walt Disney emphasized: "Disneyland is a work of love. We didn't go into Disneyland just with the idea of making money."
Walt had been called to create Disneyland:

"Disneyland really began when my two daughters were very young. Saturday was always 'Daddy's Day' and I would take them to the merry-go-round and sit on a bench eating peanuts, while they rode. And sitting there alone, I felt that something should be built, some kind of family park where parents and children could have fun together." – Walt Disney

So, my friend, I now invite you to pause and ask yourself: "Does my heartfelt intuition call me to go forth in this direction?

My heart has called me to direct feature films, create graphic novels, write and sing songs as part of a band, teach MBA students at Stanford University, write 45 books—and more.

I've answered the call again and again.

What does your heart call you to do?

Yes—there may be years in which you do a "rent job" to support yourself and race home and do your heartfelt work.

We, who adopt the plan of "Whatever it takes," step forward without regrets.

Just imagine what you might do if you quieted down fear and took some good steps forward.

Exercise #19:

Pause. Think of a tough situation you're in. Ask yourself: "Does my heartfelt intuition call me to go forth in this direction?" Write in your personal journal. Note your thoughts and feelings.

* the above section originally appeared as a blog post at
YourBodySoulandProsperity.com (with visitors from 101 countries

Use Powerful Methods for Risks and Making Big Decisions

"It's hard for me to make the big decisions," my client Cara said.

"I hear you," I replied. "That's understandable. I've been listening carefully to your current situation and you have a lot at stake."

Working with clients, and as CEO, leading my international team members for my own company, I work with people taking appropriate risks.

I recall this quote:

"Failure or the risk of failure could often be a crucial step on the road to success." – Dominic Randolph

Being skillful about "risk of failure" is valuable.

"The heart and soul of the company is creativity and innovation. ... People don't like to follow pessimists." – Bob Iger, CEO of The Walt Disney Company

I usually write about having courage and using strategy to take appropriate risks.

There is another side to this equation.

It's valuable to learn when taking a particular risk is ill-advised.

I use **3 Considerations Related to Saying "No" to a Particular Risk**

- If it's not hell yes, then it's hell no.
- I don't feel a burning energy to do this.

- If in doubt, leave it out.
- *Bonus Consideration:* Really wanting it to be true does *not* make it true.

1. "If it's not hell yes, then it's hell no."

Years ago, I saw a comment by Cheryl Richardson in one of her books: "If it's not hell yes, then it's hell no."

This is useful. Why? Because whatever you decide, you're going to pay for it. For example, years ago, I directed a feature film in which I played a leading character, and I did my own stunts.

I held onto the hood of a speeding, classic, cherry-red Chevy truck going 60 miles an hour.

Would I do that today? No. I'm *not* interested. Been there, done that. I'm older, and I'm not interested in risking great injury. I'd rather devote my time to leading my team in projects including my novel series *Jenalee Storm.*

Now it's your turn. Do you really want something? Is it a total, enthusiastic "hell yes!"? If not, then maybe it's NOT worth it to you.

2. I don't feel a burning energy to do this.

Recently, I was offered two big opportunities. Both required that I invest money and time in big proportions. I said to my sweetheart, "I don't feel a burning energy to do this." That was an important point! It's good to listen to yourself.

Now it's your turn. As you talk with people you trust about a particular risk, how do you *really* feel about it? Do you feel a burning energy to do it?

3. If in doubt, leave it out

I've made big decisions. I've led five companies—plus

directing my first feature film, giving my first big speech in front of 703 people, writing a book [I've written 45 books], hiring important team members and more.

Did I have any doubts when I went ahead? I did have a small doubt or two. But during those times, my big, positive burning desire was more important than any fear I had.

On the other hand, a Big, Important Doubt, might be your intuition saying: "Hey! Pay attention to this. Something is OFF here."

If you have that kind of doubt, "leave it out"—that is, protect yourself and don't go down a dark path.

Now it's your turn. Do you have a "Big, Important Doubt"? Is your wish for a specific outcome maybe blinding you to a big downside?

3a. *Bonus Consideration:* Really wanting it to be true does *not* make it true.

One particular time, someone invited me to join a business opportunity. When I first heard about the business situation and what MIGHT blossom out of it, my heart filled up with "Oh! I hope this is true—and this works! My life would change so much. This could be my Big Breakthrough!"

It was necessary for me to quiet down my fantasy-thoughts and take a close look at the whole situation.

I call myself an OptiRealist. That is, I'm optimistic that we can make things better *And* I'm realistic to know that strategy is necessary. Another realistic view is that any project can get bumpy or even fall apart. Maybe you could barely hold the project together, but with the wrong people involved, you could waste a lot of your time.

For example, I directed a certain film project years ago. A certain actor refused to re-record certain lines of dialogue.

This person was afraid of losing close-up shots. Wait a minute! If the scene does not make sense, this actor would still lose!

I carefully explained the need for the scenes to be re-edited to make the whole film project work. Still, this actor refused to record new lines of dialogue.

My solution: I replaced the voice of that actor through the whole film. I had to fix the scenes. That was my job as producer and film director.

A Special Consideration: *Ask yourself, "How much control do I have in the project, so I can take action to fix things?"* If you have multiple opportunities before you, you may want to focus on those projects that give you a good degree of control, so you CAN fix things.

It is realistic to understand that sometimes people will be so self-focused that they may hurt a project.

My point is: Pay close attention. If you're in a project with trustworthy people, you'll be okay. If you doubt the professionalism of people involved, it may be time to avoid the deal or situation.

Now it's your turn. Have you interviewed a lot of people related to the proposed deal or situation? Have you made sure to realize "wanting something to be true does *not* make it true"?

As an Executive Coach and the Spoken Word Strategist, I often work with clients who need to take appropriate risks. How do you know if the risk is appropriate?

One part of the process is to thoroughly submit the risky deal or situation to these **3 Considerations Related to Saying "No" to a Particular Risk**
- If It's not hell yes, then it's hell no.
- I don't feel a burning energy to do this.
- If in doubt, leave it out.

- *Bonus Consideration:* Really wanting it to be true does *not* make it true.

You really need to get access to your intuition. Some researchers identify intuition as "unconscious intelligence." That is, they suggest that you really *know* something, but it has not risen to the neocortex of the brain yet.

Pay close attention.

Guard your time and resources.

Then you can get the most value when you take an appropriate risk.

Exercise 20:

Look over these Considerations.
- If it's not hell yes, then it's hell no.
- I don't feel a burning energy to do this.
- If in doubt, leave it out.
- *Bonus Consideration:* Really wanting it to be true does *not* make it true.

Write in your personal journal and note your thoughts and feelings that arise from looking over these details.

* The above section appeared as a blog post at GetTheBigYES.com

Roi Leaders Make Great Decisions While Facing Risk #3

RoiLeaders Don't Let Fear of Disappointment Hold Them Back

"Something's holding me back," my client, Matt, said.

"What are you *not* doing?" I asked.

"I … I'm not making enough marketing phone calls," he said.

"What's that coming from?"

"People saying 'no' is hard for me to take."

"I hear you. That's rough on me, too," I said.

"I get so disappointed. I know I'm offering something of value. Still, it hurts," he said.

* * *

Have you noticed how some people just quit because they're afraid of getting disappointed? Perhaps, a lot of that arises from parents and guardians tossing off ideas like: "Do you realize how few people make a living doing that?" or "Well, don't get your hopes up. It's only a small chance that you can win." A number of parents seem to try to inoculate their kids from the pain of disappointment.

This doesn't work. Hiding from disappointment causes, in the long term, more pain.

On the other hand, I've learned to brace myself, acknowledge the possibility of real disappointment, and move forward, anyway.

This is a Hidden Secret of Success: Get into the arena, face possibilities of disappointment and move forward, anyway.

Why? Because my own mentors and role models are those

who are successful because they take more appropriate risks than others. Top, successful people confront "no" much more often than those who play it safe in "regular jobs."

I invite you to enjoy the *Power of Overcoming the Fear of Disappointment.*

We'll use the W.I.N. process:

W – wonder

I – intensify

N – network

1. Wonder

Years ago, a top Las Vegas stage hypnotist shared with me a conversation he had with a designer of stage illusions. This designer said that David Copperfield will work on twelve projects, and two will work out. The designer said that he would work on only one project until it worked. It appears that David Copperfield was succeeding nine more times per year.

When I talk about "wonder," I'm inviting you to wonder about what you could attempt.

Use the Power of Three

Consider identifying three ways to market something or three projects to work on. Having only one project can create a flood of disappointment when it does not work. However, three projects give you more chances at success. Also, three means that one does *not* stretch oneself too thin and dissipate one's energy.

If you devoted a short time to "wondering," what might you explore to be a project or way to market what you offer?

2. Intensify

If you know that what you're doing is going to likely

result in disappointment, then intensify your efforts to have more opportunities to present. By this I mean, get in front of more people.

Some time ago, I said to a team member at my company:

If you have one and you lose one, that's a tragedy.

If you lose one and you have twenty to go, that's just a step.

In dealing with the Fear of Disappointment, it's great to use strategy. Our strategy here is to fill the "funnel" with more prospective clients.

3. Network

Authors John C. Maxwell and Jim Collins write about "who luck." Jim coined this term, which refers to the old phase about "who you know."

One way to ensure that you can withstand more disappointment is to expand your horizons. It's vital to become known as a Hub of Influence. This means that individuals will connect with you because you're known for being helpful and connected to many people.

Here are two valuable questions to ask a new acquaintance:

- Who is your ideal client?
- How can I be supportive of what you're doing?

In summary, successful people take good care of themselves and make sure to stay strong so they can face rejection and disappointment every week.

Remember to:

W – wonder

I – intensify

N – network

Finally, be sure to separate in your mind these two forms of disappointment: a) External Factor Disappointment and b) Self-Disappointment.

If we do not make our marketing phone calls, we may suffer from feeling disappointment in ourselves. However, we can realize that with more efforts, we'll have more opportunities.

Recently, I said to a client: "You're making five marketing phone calls a day. That's fulfilling an *Effort-Goal*. Good work. And whether an individual says 'yes'—that's often due to external factors. Keep up your efforts, and you'll feel better. You'll be proud of yourself."

Exercise 21:

Excellent leaders are always on the lookout to increase their network.

Do these questions work for you?

- Who is your ideal client?
- How can I be supportive of what you're doing?

Use these questions or your own versions at a networking event.

Roi Leaders Make Great Decisions While Facing Risk #4

The Secret to Help You Decide and Bring in Real Success

"I know I should do this," Mark said. "But I don't think I can afford it."

The day before I had an in-depth conversation with Mark about where his business was—but more importantly, about what great things will happen when he fulfills his Own Potential and fulfills the potential of his business. Still, Mark was stuck.

As an Executive Coach, I've helped people do amazing things. What is required for that? Breaking out of your limitations involves making a shift to an Empowered Mindset.

Here are **three vital Elements of Making the Life-Changing Decision.** We'll use the W.I.N. process:

1. Wonder about "the Signs"

Pay attention. Are you saying, "I know I should do this"? Your own subconscious mind is telling you something important. You may also see things in your environment. Your brain has the Reticular Activating System (RAS). The RAS becomes sensitive to the environment. If you're thinking about buying a particular brand of car, you start seeing those cars everywhere.

Perhaps, you start seeing memes on social media about people who took the right risk and made their lives full of abundance, creativity and adventure. That's the Universe saying, "You can have wonderful things in your life, too.

Step forward in faith."

Get clear on this distinction:

The Voice of Fear says: "Contract, hide, do not take an appropriate risk."

The Voice of Intuition says: "Expand, experiment, take an appropriate risk."

Make space to hear your intuition.

2. Identify if you're scared *and* excited

Growing to a Higher Level calls on you to stretch. It is natural for you to feel some fear. In fact, in the right situation, it is required. Required? Yes. You are kicking off the mud of your Previous Chapter of Life. You're going to need to perform on a level that you've never experienced before.

If you feel scared, I'm with you. Just before I directed my first feature film, I was scared, deep in my bones. What did I do? I personally drew 801 storyboard images. I made sure that I knew the story up-down-sideways and through and through. Total preparation.

Here's something else: my co-producer said, "Tom, you play a leading role—as one of the characters." What?! My stress would already be off the charts. But I knew: Things were in place. I had the team, the script, filming equipment and a tiny budget. Our budget was too low to gain the actor we wanted. I could try to "play it safe" and wait. Or I could do what my gut and heart said: "Direct this film now. Play that character. Do NOT let this chance get away!"

I'm so glad that I took the risk. It literally changed my life! I went into different circles and met the love of my life. I even became an educator, training MBA students at Stanford University. Because I took the right risk.

What has you both scared *and* excited? Is this your Big

Chance? Find out.

Here's my phrase: To stand out, find out what you stand for.

My friend, I invite you to *Stand Up for Your New and Great Chapter of Your Own Life!*

3. Nurture and Expand Your Capabilities

Will taking this risk Increase Your Capabilities? That's the question to consider. Many of us notice that (often) we don't regret what we did. We regret what we did NOT do. Some time ago, I had little money. Still, I invested in getting coaching and taking workshops and online courses. Why? It was all about Increasing My Capabilities.

My friend: Increasing Your Capabilities is just like having gold that massively increases in value. That's right. When you expand your skills and personal experience, you have some "gold" that truly appreciates in value. You cannot go wrong.

Let's say you have the choice between getting a huge-screen TV or putting the money into some coaching. Make the decision to Increase Your Capabilities. Why? You'll be able to afford multiple TVs (if the courses you take and the coaching you get are about improving your prowess in business).

Special Note: Will the decision increase your capabilities and upgrade your circle of contacts? Recently, I attended a conference and made so many high-value connections—it was a true joy and opportunity.

Let's remember these *Vital Elements to Make the Best Decisions to Unleash Financial Abundance in Your Life:*

W – Wonder about "the Signs"

I – Identify if you're scared *and* excited

N – Nurture and expand Your Capabilities

Make better decisions.

Take an appropriate risk.

Become proud of yourself.

Exercise 22:

Does something have you both scared *and* excited? Use your personal journal to write down your thoughts and feelings.

Roi Leaders Make Great Decisions While Facing Risk #5

Get Strong, Face Risk and Achieve Your Dream

"I'm afraid," my client Sharon said. "The higher I rise; the further I have to fall."

"We'll find ways to bring your safety net up with you," I replied. We'll use the N.E.T. process:

N – nurture your resources

E – expand your plan

T – target the purpose

1. Nurture your resources.

"Nothing is impossible for the [person] who doesn't have to do it himself." – A. H. Weiler

Facing risk can be a scary time. It's vital for you to look at all your current resources and to find even more resources. You do not have to step forward by yourself.

It is helpful to develop relationships with excellent professionals before you need them.

For example, I went looking for an entertainment industry attorney before I needed her to work on projects that I was going to do in subsequent years.

Barbra Streisand, at the beginning of her career, was helped by friends who let her sleep on their couch.

Now it's your turn.

Answer these questions:

- Who can help you?
- Which professionals could assist you (attorney, accountant, financial planner, and others)?

As an Executive Coach, I often take on different roles of coach, business consultant, brand strategist, speech coach, and mentor. I currently lead teams in the United Kingdom, India and the United States of America. I have trained with my own mentors in leadership, top level speech-making and more.

I hire my own coaches and consultants so I'm constantly improving my strategic approach.

It helps for you to keep studying and reading. If reading is not your strong suit, consider listening to audio books. [My audio books are available on iTunes—*Be Heard and Be Trusted*—and my other audio book, *Darkest Secrets of Persuasion and Seduction Masters: How to Protect Yourself and Turn the Power to Good*].

2. Expand your plan

To face risk in an effective manner, look at the whole situation. Several people refer to this as "look at the whole chessboard."

Have multiple plans.

Answer these questions and write down your answers in your plans:

- What if the first phase of your project does not work? How can you recover?
- How can you minimize the damage?
- How can you go into action quickly?
- How can you keep the budget modest, so you do not risk the whole company?

The team that made $100 million with the Thighmaster product, began with a plan to develop and market eight products. The first product did not work, and Thighmaster was product #2.

Many years ago, I was flown into Utah as a finalist to be a

trainer for a top time management company. It looked like the articulate, blond woman gained that position.

Sure, I was disappointed. I did not stop. Instead, I "got on another horse."

I immediately rented a church's hall and held my own time management workshop using my own proprietary methods. The workshop started me on the path to giving six speeches at the annual conferences for the National Association of Broadcasters, Washington, D.C. And that led to my teaching graduate students and college students for over 18 years.

It's great to have multiple plans.

It's like having multiple irons in the fire because you do not know which particular iron will become red hot.

Now it's your turn. Write down an Expanded Plan.

Include:

- How you can recover if Phase One of your project does not work out.
- How you can fall back and do something else while your revise the project.
- How you can keep finances going as you develop your project.

I've interviewed a number of people who have successfully conducted crowdfunding campaigns.

One person I know raised his rent-money by offering to make a simple website for people who donated $100.00. Several people took up his offer.

Many times, a money problem can be converted into a "find another way to serve people" solution.

3. Target the purpose

When you truly connect with your purpose for a project or your "life-direction," you can be flexible and jump at multiple opportunities.

I've learned that being out in the world and finding ways to serve others brings on more opportunities.

Many years ago, I served a group of job-seekers by giving a pro bono presentation at the San Francisco Employment Development Department. I taught skills to help people develop their effective personal brand.

My purpose was to be helpful to these people who were hurting due to enduring a job loss.

One attendee came up to me and said, "You should speak for XY company." This led to over $312,000 worth of work.

Now it's your turn.

What is your purpose?

Do you want to entertain people? Can you do it as a writer, actor, singer—or some combination?

Do you want to lift people's hearts? Can you do it by giving a speech?—revising a speech for someone else?—co-writing a book?

When you're facing a risk, see if you can pause and do some strategic planning.

Take a long view. Keep looking to expand your skills and experience.

Stay active and find ways to serve.

Exercise 23:

Write down your first version of an Expanded Plan that includes these details:

- How you can recover if Phase One of your project does not work out.
- How you can fall back and do something else while your revise the project.
- How you can keep finances going as you develop your project.

PART SIX:
RoiLeaders Stay Strong

Related to Self-awareness

RoiLeaders Stay Strong #1

Achievers Rising: Avoid Burnout and Arise to New Heights of Success

"What surprised you about coaching people to big, transformational successes, Tom?" my friend Carl asked.

"Some of my clients, in the past, would hit a valley after a big success," I replied.

In recent years, I work with clients to help them be strong and avoid burnout. In fact, I use this phrase: "This is when We Get Tough."

First, we face reality. We acknowledge these Myths that arise out of what people imagine success to be:

Myths:

1. You'll feel like you have arrived.
2. You'll have no more problems.
3. No one misunderstands you.
4. You'll feel good all the time.
5. You'll stay excited all the time.
6. You'll never have any doubts that you're on the right path.
7. You'll never wonder why you feel disheartened, disorientated or disappointed (the 3 Ds).

When I speak on the topic "Achievers Rising: Avoid Burnout and Arise to New Heights of Success," I share the A.I.M. process.

A – arrange and rotate challenge, activity, recovery

I – intensify self-nurturing

M – move

1. Arrange and rotate challenge, activity, recovery

The idea is that you can get tired, but you do not let yourself get exhausted. Exhausted can be in body or spirit or both. The solution is to be deliberate about your Recovery Actions. I log my sleep, exercise daily and eat salad for breakfast (willpower is stronger earlier in the day).

Now it's your turn: What do you do to ensure you have enough Recovery in your life?

Some people fall apart when they first achieve millionaire status—including Jim Rohn and Tony Robbins. They lose big sums of money and must endure a real struggle on their way back to the top. Additionally, bestselling author and entrepreneur Randy Gage talked about how his life fell apart during some successful times.

What is the solution? Maintain structure in your daily life and rotate Challenge, Activity and Recovery.

Challenge can bring new energy into your life. One of my clients became excited about a new writing project. Some coaches might say, "Shut that down. That's a distraction."

Instead, I said, "We'll use that excitement. It will spread so you have the energy to do what you must do." We also make sure that the new project "does NOT take over."

I'm an OptiRealist. I know that optimism can provide the fuel for achievement. And still, I'm a realist. I help my clients see the whole picture and see the end game. Then we build the strategies to make positive things happen.

Energy is still crucial. I have a phrase: *What you dread gets you ahead.* In line with this principle, we realize that one needs energy to do the tough things in life.

It's the rotating of challenge, activity and recovery that helps my clients continue to soar and reach higher and higher levels of success. Remember, Challenge, Activity, Recovery. You might say: "No C.A.R.; no go."

2. Intensify self-nurturing

When I work with CEOs and business owners, I see them easily gravitate to the "shiny goals." These are goals that are fun to talk about. I call them "Golden Pull Goals." For you to avoid burnout, you need another form of goal—what I call Green Tranquility Goals. These are "Being Goals." On a daily basis, you do something that strengthens you. My clients use activities like quiet time, meditation, painting, journaling, praying, walking near trees, watching something funny on video (enjoying laughter everyday), yoga, tai chi, and other nurturing actions.

For my clients who are introverts, I help them put some quiet time into their daily lives. They must recharge while they are alone—away from other people. For an introvert, being with other people is expensive in terms of personal energy.

Additionally, I guide my clients to avoid the "After a Success, a fall into a valley." The solution is to overlap one's goals. Here's an example. Before I finished my 35th book, I started writing my first novel. I did not fall into a post-project spot of emptiness.

Now it's your turn. Find out what nurtures your feelings of fulfillment. When do you feel creative and on track? How can you "overlap your goals"?

3. Move

"Don't worry about it. I'm just procrastinating a bit and trying to find clarity," Sarah, my client said.

"I hear you," I replied. We talked for a bit more. Then, I shared this: "**Motion brings clarity.** Try things. Get in the arena. See how things feel."

I added, "You get to the top of a peak and then you can see three new peaks (new choices). You couldn't see the choices when you were not in motion and you were at the bottom of the mountain."

The most successful people I've interviewed get into the arena where they can face rejection and failure—much more than other people.

After I give certain speeches, some business owners come up to me and say, "I just need to find the right salesperson." A bit later in the conversation, I mention: "How can you train a salesperson if you don't know what works? People like to join successful ventures. You need to get involved in sales and marketing. You need to develop the pitch (and really a good dialogue) and watch people's faces. Founders of companies do well when they learn to sell what they're offering. They learn to use compelling stories."

When I say "move"—I mean Get in Motion. Learn, rehearse, practice, get coaching, get in front of potential customers/clients.

A powerful part of "Move" is to Shift Your Perception

For example, we avoid burnout when we drop certain expectations. Success is NOT static. We do not simply "arrive."

I've learned that Connecting to the Present Moment is crucial.

It's helpful to realize that this is an AND-Universe. [I

wrote a book titled, *The Hidden Power of the AND-Universe*.]

Here are brief comments about Shifting Your Perception:
a) You can be Grateful *and* feel uncomfortable.

For example, as I write these words, I'm grateful to be connecting with you. *And*, I'm in pain. I recently broke a tooth (on a soft cookie—oh, the irony).

Still, I avoid wallowing in the pain. I shift my thoughts to so much in my life that I'm grateful for now.

You can also be grateful for what is absent. I have a couple of friends who tried to talk me out of writing a lot of books. They drifted away. What a relief! An old phrase holds: Some people brighten a room by leaving it.

b) Experience the Shift in Perspective that Opens the World to You

Imagine the possibilities when you shift away from fear to intuition. First, let's look at the differences:

Fear says, "Contract, hide, don't take any risks."

Intuition says, "Expand, experiment, take an appropriate risk."

Life becomes an adventure when we're *not* shackled by fear.

"If you do something that scares you, it is often coming from a place that might create a button [an impact on the audience]."
– Leonard Nimoy
"The universe often rewards us for the scary choices."
– Pharrell Williams

c) Discover the Power of Enjoying the Moments as they come and go.

"Your task is not to seek for love, but merely to seek and find all the barriers within yourself that you have built against it." – Rumi

I've learned that removing the barriers to being fully alive in this present moment is the vital difference that helps an achiever keep on achieving—and to avoid burnout.

My successful clients (and those whom I interview) also discover the value in helping others and turning their focus away from their own personal concerns. Burnout often arises when we get caught up in personal frustrations. Years ago, I knew someone who would go into a rage when he had "a bad workout." He said, "My day is ruined." At that time, I remembered an old phrase: "You're upset because your canvas is too small."

Instead, we can expand the canvas of our life when we're engaged with demonstrating kindness to others. For example, in my book, *What the Rich Don't Say about Getting Rich*, I interview Michael Hsieh (president of a venture capital fund) who shares his delight in supporting children with few resources to have access to an extraordinary education (at a chartered school).

Be sure to include a focus on something beyond yourself.

Remember to use the A.I.M. process:

A – arrange and rotate challenge, activity, recovery

I – intensify self-nurturing

M – move

Earlier, I mentioned, *Success is not static.*

Pay close attention to how your life is going.

Rotate challenge, activity and recovery so that you'll continue to soar and reach higher and higher levels of success.

Exercise 24:

How can you intensify your self-nurturing? Write down 9 ideas in your personal journal.

RoiLeaders Stay Strong #2

Move Ahead Successfully Even When You're Criticized

Do you want real success and fulfillment? Then, learn to handle criticism in an empowered manner. The crucial detail when facing criticism is to prepare to answer your own personal and empowering questions.

1. Does this person really want good things for me?
2. What are my personal goals and does this comment strengthen me?
3. Does this comment strengthen my work?
4. Does this comment help me learn and grow?

1. Does this person really want good things for me?

I have an extended family member who has nothing but criticism for me. He's older and he's never been an entrepreneur, author, educator or feature film director. Those are my areas of expertise. However, this person just wants to make me "wrong." Wait a minute! This is a family member, but his goal is "to be right" and "to put the other person down." It's sad really.

When you consider whether criticism has merit, consider the source. If someone is in your target market, that criticism may be useful. However, if someone is merely guessing and has never entered the field you're working in, assess whether to dismiss such criticism.

Talking to my negative extended family member would be where good ideas go to die. So, I often avoid this person. I have a circle of friends and colleagues who are supportive and still provide me with the constructive feedback that may be hard to hear, but their intention is good things for me. I can trust them.

2. What are my personal goals and does this comment strengthen me?

What are your real goals? Do you want to be famous? Do you want to do good artistic work? Do you want to make lots of money? Do you deeply long to express your creativity?

All the above have different elements attached to them.

It's important for you to be honest with yourself. What do you really want?

The truth is that I want to serve my readers, audiences, graduate students and clients. So, I'm willing to hear tough feedback and learn about areas to improve for my projects. For each book I write, I test the material with multiple people. They can be really tough, and they push me to write in better ways. That's what I really want. I do *not* want to be coddled.

So even if my editors might occasionally clothe a comment with sarcasm, I still know that their comments actually strengthen me. After writing 45 books, I'm a better writer today.

Also, pause and get access to your own intuition. Often, some people are so quick to judge and say, "That won't work." How do they know? And imagine this: If your intuition is correct and you follow your heart—and you succeed—what will they say? They'll merely shrug and mildly reply, "Oh, I guess I was wrong on that one." Do *not* leave your fate to someone else. Answer your own heart's call.

To take this conversation to the next step, you can view my 7-min. video "How to Believe in Yourself When Others Don't" on YouTube.com. Type "Tom Marcoux believe."

3. Does this comment strengthen my work?

This is where the real work takes place. A tough comment like "I think that totally fails to engage your target market" may be the best reality check that you need. For example, with a video related to my science fiction franchise *TimePulse*, my team hit a wall. We needed a paragraph to bridge two sections of the video. I had four people tell me that the paragraph missed the mark. Okay. Back to the drawing board. Eventually, we came up with a solution. With a new approach, we found an appropriate quote to bridge the sections.

4. Does this comment help me learn and grow?

My team members know that I can calmly listen to any comment that points out flaws in a draft of a project. I'll often ask follow-up questions. Why? I'm focused on learning and growing as an artist in the various fields I participate in: speaking, writing, filmmaking and art direction of graphic novels.

My point is that a truly creative person must develop a "thick skin" and run criticism through a filter. Some critical comments have nothing to do with your goals. Let them flow past like leaves on a stream of water.

Other comments, which are given to support you, and which strengthen your work, may raise your work to world-class level. It's an adventure that is actually worth the pain and effort. It's a road that includes surprising, happy moments.

Exercise 25:

Consider the criticism you're getting now.

Analyze what the person's approach is.

Ask yourself:

1. Does this person really want good things for me?
2. What are my personal goals and does this comment strengthen me?
3. Does this comment strengthen my work?
4. Does this comment help me learn and grow?

RoiLeaders Stay Strong #3

How to Believe in Yourself When Others Don't

"He sold all of his furniture-making equipment and then later they got a divorce," one of my friends said about his brother.

This story revealed the poison some people spew around. The brother had been hit twice: First, his then-wife had *not* believed in him to the point of pushing him to give up his hobby and business. Second, his wife left him. So, the unbeliever had left after having done damage.

Actually, the divorce might ultimately open the door to a brighter, better chapter in the brother's life.

This story serves as a cautionary tale. *We need to be advocates for ourselves.*

Upon reflection, I thought about what gets in the way of our *Expressing Our Light.*

1. Others drown out our Heartfelt Voice

The answer is: *Acknowledge it's your destiny and NOT theirs.*

Here's a way you can stay strong even when you feel all alone and deeply disappointed that loved ones do *not* support you in your making your dream come true.

Perhaps, like many people, your loved ones are afraid. Maybe on a subconscious level they're afraid that you'll get hurt as you step out of your comfort zone. Or even, they feel uncomfortable being around someone so focused and striving to fulfill his or her potential. Maybe they fear that you'll change and leave them behind when you do succeed on a significant scale. Sometimes we lose friends. Top author and speaker Larry Winget wrote: "Some friendships are like belts. We outgrow them."

Here's an important point to realize: Other people cannot feel what you feel or intuitively know what you know. Why? It is *your* destiny—not their destiny. You're the one person who has all the clues and internal signs that your idea is a valuable one.

Perhaps, you've felt the gut-wrenching disappointment when a loved one does *not* support you in your pursuit of something that's close to your heart.

Here's an answer that I learned from my neighbor who races motorcycles competitively. He said, "In motorcycle racing, we're trained with the idea: If in doubt, gas it out." The idea is to "pour on the gas." My neighbor assures me that if there's an irregularity in the road, more gas will help the motorcyclist get over the small ridge.

How can we apply *if in doubt, gas it out?* First, look to yourself for confirmation and energy. Add things that empower you. Often, when I'm writing I'm listening to empowering music. I read empowering books, and I see uplifting films.

The point here is: *You must take action to keep up your own spirits.*

2. Fear strangles Your Connection with Your Intuition.
The answer is: *Identify with your intuition*

Above, I invited you to listen to yourself for confirmation.

Just because someone close to you cannot see or imagine your idea that does *not* mean that they're right! It just means that they cannot feel the value of your idea.

Identify with your intuition and *not* their fears.

Many things that turned out well took time. For example, it took eight years and many studios turning down the feature film *Splash* before it was produced, and Ron Howard directed the film. In fact, Disney turned it down the first time, and it was not until Disney created a new division, Touchstone Pictures, did *Splash* (starring Tom Hanks and Darryl Hannah) get made.

A truly famous example is how co-authors Mark Victor Hansen and Jack Canfield held to their intuition and endured 140 rejections before their book *Chicken Soup for the Soul* was published. The *Chicken Soup for the Soul* series has resulted in 250 titles and more than 500 million books sold.

Go by your intuition. Do not rely on others to "have all the answers." So-called experts can be wrong. You may be providing something that is new and different.

How can you recognize your "voice of intuition"?

Here's a quick description of two "voices."

- *Voice of fear:* contract, hide, do not experiment
- *Voice of intuition:* expand, build, take appropriate risks

Every day and really every moment, we have a choice. Do we grow and expand and step toward our destiny? Or do we contract and hide and let doubters bring us down?

I invite you to nurture yourself and step forward in a steady pace to create new and better in your life.

3. Your fear of loss of approval has you hide your light.

The answer is: *Measure by your heart and NOT their approval.*

In a way, I've been lucky that my father is stuck, for decades, in a disapproval mode. I've learned to listen to my own heart and ignore his negativity. The truth is he has had no experience related to being an entrepreneur, graduate school instructor, author, and feature film director. Sure, he has opinions—uninformed opinions. And I'm so glad that I ignored his narrow-viewed advice. My life has been so much more of a joyful adventure than merely playing it safe. His constant refrain is "survival." I've replied, "That's not enough. I want to thrive!"

Do you have someone close to you who simply does not support your vision?

Walt Disney's own wife, brother/business partner and board of directors were all against Disneyland. Why? There had never been a theme park before. In fact, Walt's wife Lillian asked Walt, "Why do you want to do an amusement park? They're so dirty." Walt replied, "Mine will be clean!"

Walt measured things by his own heart. In fact, his first thoughts about creating an amusement park began in 1911 when, as children, he and his sister would stand outside the gates of a Kansas City amusement park. It was not until 1955 when he opened his own gates of Disneyland. Can you hold onto an idea for 44 years? Will you take steady steps forward?

Novelist Greg Bear told me that it took 10 years for readers to discover one of his novels.

My point is that some dreams take several years—and several starts and stops and moments or months of discouragement.

Plenty of people, often those closest to us, will express their doubt. As emphasized in this section, it's only natural because you are the one who hears your personal and unique "music and vision."

Nurture yourself and your vision.

Get coaching and continue your efforts to learn more and more.

This world needs people who hold to their vision and

persist. Thank you!

Exercise 26:

Is there someone near you who is holding you back? Do drown out our Heartfelt Voice?

Acknowledge it's your destiny and NOT theirs. Write down your thoughts and feelings. How will you empower yourself?

Tom Marcoux

RoiLeaders Stay Strong #4

RoiLeader Explores True Confidence

What is confidence? Is it when you feel comfortable enough to do something different?
No.

Confidence is <u>not</u> comfort. Confidence is a toolkit, and you work it. – Tom Marcoux

I coach my clients and MBA students in something I call *Extreme Confidence.*

Extreme Confidence is when you KNOW that you know how to adapt to anything the arises.

Such confidence is built on strategy, positive philosophy and rehearsal.

Confidently Connect with People even when You Feel Like You're Failing

"How can I genuinely connect with people even when deep inside I feel like I'm failing?" my client, Alisha, asked.
"What brings this up?" I asked.
"I feel like I'm not making enough marketing calls. I feel ashamed about that. I even feel scared," Alisha said.
I next guided her in the process **Shift to an Empowering Question.** The idea is that we shift out of dark thoughts into

new, positive possibilities.

First, I'll share that successful people I've interviewed and those I've studied find that just before the breakthrough there is a "breakdown"—that is big trouble. For example, Denis Waitley wrote *The Psychology of Winning* when he was flat broke. He finished that audio program, and it went on to be one of the bestselling audio programs of all time.

Years ago, some authors wrote: "Fake it until you make it."

On the other hand, I have something better for you: **Act It Until You Become It.**

We're *not* talking about trying to prevent every negative thought. Instead, we're talking about *Shifting to an Empowering Question.*

Use the Power of "How can I …?"

Here's an example: "How can I take what I learned on that sales call, and do better with the next one?"

I'll answer that. Write things down and keep notes. For every sales call, you can use what I share with my clients: In a journal, you draw a line down the center of the page. On the left side, write down: "What worked." On the right side, write down "Areas to Improve."

The idea is to capture that information. That's how you're going to do better.

Use the Power of "How can we …?"

The focus is on "we." For example, when I guide clients to identify *3 Levels of Goals: Good, Excellent, and Amazing!,* we note that Amazing Results require a team or at least connections with other people.

One of my clients applied this "How can we?" process.

She asked, "How can we … get me more referrals?"

That was a great starting point.

In summary, we're talking about how a negative thought comes up—and your effective response is to come back with an Empowering Question.

Here's another Empowering Question: How can I take one small step now in a positive direction?

If you're worried about failing to make enough marketing phone calls, you ask, "How can I change my schedule?" One of my mentors emphasizes "8 before 8"—that is, 8 phone calls before 8 in the morning. He also says, "5 after 5." That is, 5 phone calls after 5 PM in the evening.

Remember, when a negative thought comes up, you ask an Empowering Question.

So, if you're about to give a sales presentation or speech, ask yourself: "How can I help these people?"—"How can I listen well and help them know I care?"—"How may I serve?"

You'll feel better. You'll go into action.

Once in action, you'll feel more confident. In this way, you can do better with your meetings/conversations during the day.

Exercise 27:

Who can you talk with and use the "How can we...?" process. Perhaps, certain trusted friends can offer you new perspectives. Perhaps, it's time to hire an executive coach.

RoiLeaders Stay Strong #5

How You Can Persevere and Achieve Great Success

"What is something true that took you by surprise?" my friend, Alana, asked.

"I've frequently observed something in clients. They run into the 'After a Big Leap Crash,'" I said.

"What's that?"

"The client works hard and accomplishes something significant. First book completed. First speech at a conference. Then the person slows down," I said.

"What's that about?" Alana asked.

I went on to mention that each individual is different. Still, some patterns emerge. Different spiritual paths and psychological observations refer to one's "ego"—that part of us which is made of fear.

When one accomplishes something that is life-changing, the ego acts up and works like a spring to pull one backwards.

One time, I mentioned to a client, "We need to be careful about the After a Big Leap Crash because it can ignite the 'house' and burn it down."

The Good News in the Face of the *After a Big Leap Crash*

The Crash can be shorter in duration and severity. We can take action to avoid the "house burning down."

How?

I help the client put in the 3 *Rs*—*Reset, Renew, Roll*

Forward.

Let's look at each element in turn.

Reset

Going full speed with little sleep is *not* sustainable. So, Reset can include changing one's sleeping and exercise habits. For example, I guided a client to move her meditation period and her "tapping the heart chakra" period to earlier in the evening. These two practices were keeping her awake later into the night.

Renew

After you have achieved a big thing, you have a new project that we call "Renew Myself." You might need to explore a couple of new things like tai chi, a new hobby, or a dance class with one's spouse. You have given a lot of energy "at the office." Now, it's time to bring in new experiences and manifest new energy for your well-being.

Roll Forward

Some people notice a form of "life's irony." You've attained a new level of success. Now is the time to really take advantage of the new opportunities. You have now entered the Season of Harvest.

But then, some of my clients say, "But I do not have the energy to seize all the opportunities." First, we become selective. I emphasize *The Power of Three.* What three new opportunities are most important for you?

Second, put in place how you can "roll forward" (like a car rolling down an incline) without a big push on your part. It helps to develop positive relationships, which is sometimes called "The 10 Friends." The idea is that you can still make progress through the kind support of your inner circle friends.

With support, you do *not* have to keep racing forward.

Third, put in New Systems so you can streamline your life. For example, when I connect with a new person, I tend to send a follow-up email immediately on disconnecting the phone line. I save myself so much stress by getting the email done automatically. Less things remain as tasks "hanging over my head."

Often, clients engage me to help them put in Systems to improve their productivity and reduce their stress level.

The 3 Rs for the Foundation for "Your New Story"

When clients keep saying the same story of woe and pain, I say, "I'm looking forward to when you express a new story—which is about your 'here and now.'"

Part of the After a Big Leap Crash is something surprising: One experiences a few expectations going unfulfilled. What?

Here are some unfulfilled expectations:
- I thought with all the new income, my money worries would all vanish.
- I expected that I wouldn't have to sell every week—anymore.
- I expected that I would feel that I have finally "arrived."

Here's the Secret: Make Your New Story Incorporate Your Big Leap and Your Unexpected Experience with the Feelings

Your New Story includes three vital elements:
- Replace your pain-comment with an appreciation/new focus comment.

- Acknowledge which expectations did not turn out the way you preferred
- Create the Value and Meaning of Your Big Leap – as the Foundation for Your New Focus and Good Experiences

1) Replace your pain-comment with an appreciation/new focus comment.

I recall this classic quote:

Before enlightenment, chop wood—carry water.

After enlightenment, chop wood—carry water.

My point in sharing this quote is to acknowledge that a Big Leap often does not take all distress or discomfort out of our working activities.

The solution is to do a form of Reset. Use this pattern "Before ___; Now _____."

Here's an example:

Before I couldn't settle down to rest.

Now, I have new things in place: a) All electronics off 30 minutes before sleep, b) I use a special lightbulb (without blue wavelengths) and read just a couple paragraphs in a paperback book before I sleep, and c) I use an alarm clock— not my smartphone to wake up.

2) Acknowledge which expectations did not turn out the way you preferred

My clients discover that whatever expectations they held for the Big Leap do not match the real-life experience. Things just turn out differently.

Use this pattern: I would have preferred that _____ happened. Okay. It didn't. Here's what I learned ___. Here are the benefits I've received _____."

3) Create the Value and Meaning of Your Big Leap—as the Foundation for Your New Focus and Good Experiences

The good news is that we are meaning-creating beings. We can choose to focus on the positive.

Use this pattern:

My Big Leap has meant _____ for me and my life.

Now, from the level my Big Leap has given me, I can do _____.

If you ever find yourself telling a "poor me" story about what your Big Leap did not give you, make a shift by using these words: "The good news is _____." You can add something like: "Now that I can _____, I'm going to _____."

In summary, when you create a New, Empowering Story, you can limit the severity and duration of an After a Big Leap Crash.

Remember to focus on Reset, Renew and Roll Forward.

Exercise 28:

What resonates with you more—Reset, Renew or Roll Forward?

In what parts of your life do you need to take a new approach? Note your thoughts and feelings in your personal journal.

Tom Marcoux

Bonus Material #1

Related to Self-awareness and Relational Transparency

The Savvy CEO: Master of Media Appearances

In my speech *The Savvy CEO: Master of Media Appearances*, I share several insights related to:

- Experience Real Confidence
- Seize the Audience's Attention
- Answer Tough Questions with Poise
- Let Go of Fear and Nervousness
- Confident Body Language and Skills to Shift Topics
- Handle Tough Moments (even if your mind goes blank)

Here we'll cover a brief overview as embodied in the S.A.V.V.Y. process:

S – story
A – attention
V – vulnerability
V – victory
Y – yearning

1. Story

With storytelling, we truly connect with audience members.

In my book, *Relax, You Don't Have to Sell*, I shared the S.T.O.R.Y. process which includes:

S – set how we like the hero

T – target the hero's goal

O – open with a grabber

R – reveal the struggle

Y – yearn for the Triumphant Ending and "What I learned…"

To get the full benefit from storytelling, it's necessary to carefully structure your story. Ultimately, we're seeking to grab the audience's attention and to move their feelings.

2. Attention

A key to quieting down your nervousness is to *pay attention to your audience members*. What material is connecting with them? What is their body language conveying?

When I first began speaking, my right leg fluttered like a hummingbird's wings. I overcame this situation by *shifting* from "How am I doing?" to a new focus on the audience— "How are YOU doing?"

The idea is shift from self-consciousness to audience awareness.

3. Vulnerability

"Vulnerable?" my new client, Sam, asked. "I don't get that. The company, the board of directors requires me to be strong and clear in my objectives."

"When dealing with the media or in an all-hands speech, it helps to show you are a human being and not just a stuffed shirt," I replied.

"How do I do that?"

"We pick something that is an Appropriate Vulnerability." I went on to share how, in his later years, Dr.

Wayne Dyer warmed up the audience by talking about how his teenaged daughter would lightly poke at him by putting her hands on her hips and say: "Daaad, you know that …"

Being vulnerable in an appropriate manner wins you the connection with the audience.

4. Victory

Audiences love a well-earned victory. Somewhere in your presentation, show the goal, the setbacks and the real struggle. Then, when you express the Triumphant Outcome, the audience celebrates *with* you. You take them on the journey, so the victory feels like their victory, too.

5. Yearning

Make a real connection with an audience by connecting with their *Secret Desires*—what they're yearning for.

For example, I was working with a client. She serves women in the second half of their lives. One Secret Desire is to avoid feeling alone. So, for the description of an event, I added the detail: "Adrianna finds that women often start new, lifelong friendships at her retreats and events."

I chose the term *Secret Desires* with care because many people often hold these details close to the vest.

Here is a partial list of Secret Desires:
a) Not to be alone
b) Not to appear stupid (analytical individuals including engineers and accountants demonstrate this desire)
c) Not to be vulnerable
d) Not to be obsolete
e) Not to fall into financial ruin

We can note *Secrets Desires* in a positive way: smart, attractive, successful and rich (for example).

Researchers note *people's deep desire to be appreciated and recognized.*

Somewhere in your speech, you can include words like: "By your applause about that detail, I realize that you have your fingers on the pulse. You're really sharp to notice that …"

Pay close attention to your rapport with audience. A bit of praise goes a long way for warming up your connection with your audience.

In summary, to connect with your audience effectively, remember to be S.A.V.V.Y.:

S – story
A – attention
V – vulnerability
V – victory
Y – yearning

Exercise 29:

Develop a story so you can more vividly communicate an idea or new initiative to your team.

Remember the elements of a good story:

S – set how we like the hero
T – target the hero's goal
O – open with a grabber
R – reveal the struggle
Y – yearn for the Triumphant Ending and "What I learned…"

Bonus Material #2:

The RoiLeader and Persuasion

"All this talk about techniques … I don't see any difference between persuasion and manipulation," one of my MBA students said, during my class at Stanford University about communication skills.

I see his concern. Along this line … Years ago, I came across this quote.

"People will do anything for those who encourage their dreams, justify their failures, allay their fears, confirm their suspicions, and help them throw rocks at their enemies." – Blair Warren

At first glance, some managers/leaders might see the above ideas as part of "being influential."

I pause and say, "We're missing some vital elements:
- Respect people.
- Listen to them.
- Guide them and support them in their higher aspirations and fulfillment."

My response to the MBA student was to talk about a particular distinction:

Persuasion is good because you hold the well-being of your listener in mind.

Manipulation is bad because you're merely pulling strings on the listener with no concern for his or her well-being.

My point here is: Intent and benevolent action count.

As a professional speaker, I'm approached often by people with products they want me to sell.

I only get involved with projects that I can personally see how people will greatly benefit.

As Walt Disney said:

"Disneyland is the result of love. We did not go into Disneyland to make money." – Walt Disney

Disneyland was built on Core Values. As I've mentioned, those values were codified in 1965 by Van France as Safety, Courtesy, Show and Efficiency (first known as Capacity).

Holding to Core Values serves as one of the foundational pillars of Authentic Leadership.

Years ago, I wrote in my book *Be Heard and Be Trusted:*
"I can't persuade you if I don't know you."

That was a springboard to the idea of asking good questions and listening well.

I even wrote: "When you're listening, you're winning."

I note that without heart, the Blair Warren techniques can descend into manipulation.

The Blair Warren techniques help you *get the attention* of the listener. Okay. So, now how will you *lead?*

A friend said, "Good leaders help people get what they want." I replied, "Okay. And I'd say that good leaders help people get they want PLUS." **Plus** guiding them and supporting them in their higher aspirations and fulfillment. **Plus** guiding them to accomplish, with a team, a cause greater than the self.

We recall this quote:

"It's all about finding and hiring people smarter than you, getting them to join your business and giving them good work, then getting out of the way and trusting them. You have to get out of the way so you can focus on the bigger vision. That's important, but here is the main thing: You must make them see their work as a mission." – Richard Branson

When you start from a solid foundation of doing good—for the team member, for the customers, for the community, for the environment, and for the world, *hesitation about persuasion can drop away.*

Persuasion is about supporting the well-being of the listener.

Exercise 30:

Remember: "I can't persuade you if I don't know you." List 5 Questions that can help you learn more about the person's situation and values. Consider the question: "What's most important to you about _____?"

Tom Marcoux

Bonus Material #3

How You Can Leap Up for More Success and Happiness

"What's absolutely crucial to achieve success?" Marina, an audience member, asked me.

"Two things. How you handle fear and how you create energy in yourself," I replied.

As Spoken Word Strategist and Executive Coach, I recently helped clients manifest more energy and focus to get things done. The truth is: We need to become more skillful and take action.

Improve Your Skills related to Success, Happiness and Fear

In a number of my books, I've written about …

"When you're in action, you're focused, and fear is a quiet voice in the background." – Tom Marcoux

While I do meditate (briefly) each day, I note that my clients and I just need to get fear to quiet down—and we can move forward effectively.

(Sure, a monk, with meditating six hours a day, may eliminate most fear. Still, I'm interested in working with you in the here and now!)

Unchecked, fear can paralyze people. Fear can suck the air out of the room.

Instead, we focus on generating empowering energy.

This relates to one of my favorite quotes:

"Courage is not the absence of fear but rather the judgment that

something is more important than fear." – Meg Cabot.

My own wife elaborated on this idea. She said, "Tom, if you were in trouble, and I was scared to go over there—I'd still go over there because you're more important."

I immediately gave her a kiss and hug.

How Can You Manifest Your Courage?

Focus on what is meaningful to you—something that is more important to you than fear.

Now it's your turn. Write down your answers to these questions: "What's most important to me? What means more to me than something that scares me?

Let's Look at the Connection Between Meaning and Happiness

Think about it. Where can you derive empowering energy? It comes from what you find meaningful. (If you do something meaningful, you have a source of happiness and good feelings.)

"High Performers spend more of their time doing things that they find meaningful and this makes them happy."

– Brendon Burchard

I truly appreciate how the above comment emphasizes both focus (on the meaningful) and action. For example, every day, I write portions of my trilogy of novels, *Jenalee Storm.* This makes me happy.

Perhaps, you've noticed that several individuals focus on comfort and safety.

On the other hand, have you observed that excited people are stretching, growing and learning? Again, this is about focus, meaning and action—on the path of success and happiness. And, while you're in action, you're focused, and fear is a quiet voice in the background.

Success as a Daily Path

"Success is nothing more than a few simple disciplines, practiced every day." – Jim Rohn

"Success isn't always about greatness. It's about consistency. Consistent hard work leads to success. Greatness will come."
– Dwayne Johnson

I appreciate Dwayne Johnson's comment because it helps us let go of doubt that we may not have been "gifted" or "born great." Instead, the successful path is one of consistent hard (and focused) work.

Now it's your turn. Write down your answers to these questions: What can I do daily that connects to what I find most meaningful? How can these actions improve my skills and move my life forward?

In summary, we're noticing that success, happiness and fear do relate in certain ways to each other.

Our answer is to take daily action that is Meaningful, Makes Better Skills, and Moves Your Life Forward. (The 3 M's).

Exercise 31:

How can you spend more time doing things that are personally meaningful? Are you happy? What can you shift in your life to get you more moments of happiness in your daily life? Note your ideas in your personal journal.

Bonus Material #4 Honor Your Personal Life:

"In the end, as a leader, you are always going to get a combination of two things: what you create and what you allow."
– Henry Cloud

Are you allowing your personal life and your personal well-being to slide?

"If you don't have peace, it isn't because someone took it from you; you gave it away. You cannot always control what happens to you, but you can control what happens in you."
– John C. Maxwell

"I ride a bike and use aerobic equipment twice a week, and work out with a trainer, lifting weights." – Bob Iger, CEO of The Walt Disney Company

"The secret of your future is hidden in your daily routine."
– Mike Murdock

Do you have "non-negotiable" daily positive habits that maintain your personal well-being?

Do you have daily positive habits that support your most important relationships. For example, my wife and I have a daily walk that supports our relationship and health. Sometimes, we take multiple short walks.

Some time ago, a friend, Michelle, talked about what she was looking for in a life partner. She asked me to offer some thoughts. I said, "Look for someone who is kind and flexible."

This has me thinking about how I can stay kind and flexible. For example, I keep a log of my sleep, and I take action to get more sleep when appropriate. I log my daily exercise, quiet time and my routine that includes breathing plus a dash of tai chi and yoga.

How about you? How are taking care of yourself?

*You're making this up so make it work for you.**

What's meaningful to you?

What's important to you?

What is your purpose?

If you find yourself leaning toward negative, compulsive behaviors, *shift to ones that keep you healthy.* Get all the support and help that you need from medical personnel, an executive coach, a therapist and more.

"If you had a million-dollar racehorse, would you let him stay up half the night drinking coffee and booze, smoking cigarettes and eating junk food? ... If you did keep that million-dollar racehorse up all night smoking and drinking, how many races would he win?"– Zig Ziglar

Exercise 32:

How can you strengthen yourself by improving your daily personal activities? Do you need to modify your daily habits to include exercise, quiet time, a walk with your spouse/loved one?

---

* You're making up the elements of your life and your interpretation. We even make up many of the things that we perceive are limits. Sure, there are some real limits: For example, I do not have the physical form to be good at basketball. However, I held fears about directing films, speaking before an audience of 703 people, being the lead singer of a band and writing books—I've made accomplishments in these areas. I have exceeded the limits placed by fears. How about you? What areas to you want to go into? What coaching do you need?

A Final Word and the Springboard to Your Dreams

Congratulations on your efforts with this book.

Please consider continuing to work with me through my **executive coaching** (phone and in-person), workshops and keynote addresses. Visit my blogs:

PitchPowerFest.com

GettheBigYES.com

TheRoiLeader.com

TheSavvyCEOWins.com

YourBodySoulandProsperity.com

Meanwhile, *to get even more value from this book*, take the plans and insights that you created and place them in some form in your calendar or day planner. *Plan and take action*. Return to these pages again and again to reconnect with the material and take your life to higher levels.

The best to you,

Tom

Tom Marcoux

Spoken Word Strategist

Executive Coach—Pitch Coach

Special Offer Just for Readers of this Book:

Contact Tom Marcoux at tomsupercoach@gmail.com for special discounts on **coaching**, books, workshops and presentations. Just mention your experience with this book.

Apply for a <u>FREE Breakthrough Strategy Session</u>—see the VIDEO at TomSuperCoach.com/breakthrough

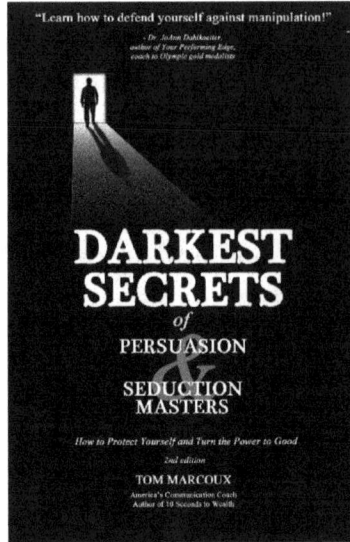

Excerpt from
Darkest Secrets of Persuasion and Seduction Masters: How to Protect Yourself and Turn the Power to Good
by Tom Marcoux, Executive Coach – Spoken Word Strategist
Copyright Tom Marcoux

. . . Now, I am in my 40's, with gray in my hair, and for 27 years I have been taking action to protect people.

And now is the time for me to protect you with the Countermeasures I reveal in this book.

Every human being needs to be able to break the trance that a Manipulator creates. You need to make good decisions so you are safe and you keep growing—and you are not cut down and crippled.

This Darkest Secrets material is so intense that I first released it only with the counterbalance of my most energizing and uplifting books, *Soar! Nothing Can Stop You This Year* and *Year of Awesome: How You Can Use 12 Success Principles including 10 Seconds to Wealth.*

An interviewer asked me: "Who can be the Manipulator?"

A co-worker, a boss, a salesperson, someone you're dating, and someone you think is a friend.

Now is the time—this very minute—for me to write this book to protect you.

I must speak the truth.

These Darkest Secrets of "persuasion masters" are …

Wait a minute! Let's say it plainly: These are the Darkest Secrets of masters of manipulation. Throughout this book, I will call these people what they are: Manipulators.

Dictionary.com defines "manipulate" as "To influence or manage shrewdly or deviously…. To tamper with or falsify for personal gain."

In this book, we will look on a manipulator as one who deviously influences someone with no concern about that person's well-being, and who causes harm to that person.

Here is the first Darkest Secret:

Darkest Secret #1:
Manipulators Make You Hurt
and Then Offer the Salve.

Manipulators would invite you to go out in the sun for hours and then sell you the salve to soothe your burns. The problem is that we don't notice that this is what they're doing.

For example, you're considering the purchase of a house. A Manipulator asks the question, "So, where would you put your TV?" This question is designed to put you into a trance.

Dictionary.com defines "trance" as "a half-conscious state, seemingly between sleeping and waking, in which ability to function voluntarily may be suspended." Let's condense this: in a trance, you may not be able to function freely.

Here is the second Secret:

Darkest Secret #2:
Manipulators Put You into a Trance.

To protect yourself, you must learn to use Countermeasures to Break the Trance.

All the Countermeasures (actions you can take to break the trance) in this book will make you stronger and more capable of protecting yourself.

Now, we'll view the third Secret:

Darkest Secret #3:
Manipulators Care Nothing for You and Human Decency: They'll lie, cheat, and do whatever they need to do so they win—but their charm masks all this.

Let's return to the example of a Manipulator selling you a house. A Manipulator does not pause for an instant to see if you can truly afford the new house. The Manipulator would neglect to mention that you will not only have your mortgage payment of $900. There will be additional costs: home repairs, property tax, water, electricity, homeowner's insurance, and more. The Manipulator only emphasizes what he or she knows you want to hear: "Look! $900 is better than the $1500 you're paying for rent, which is just going down the toilet. And the $900 is an investment."

Let's go back to **Darkest Secret #1:**

Manipulators make you hurt and then offer the salve.

The Manipulator has you feeling good about the solution (salve) and feeling bad about your current life situation.

How? A Manipulator will make you hurt through questions such as:

• What bothers you about paying $1500 a month for rent? (The Manipulator will use a derisive tone when he says the word rent.)

• What is not smart about paying rent on someone else's house instead of investing in your own house?

• How do you feel about your children walking in the neighborhood where you live now?

Do you see how these questions are designed to make you hurt enough so that you'll buy?

An interviewer asked me, "Tom, aren't these good arguments for purchasing a house?"

"What we're looking at is the *intention* of the influencer," I replied. "Let's look at our definition of a manipulator as one who deviously influences someone with no concern about that person's well-being, and who causes harm to that person. If the person truly cannot afford the house, he or she will be harmed by buying it. If the manipulator conceals the truth, the manipulator is doing harm. That's the important difference."

Some friends of mine are ethical and helpful real estate agents who truthfully reveal the whole situation and help the purchaser achieve her own goals.

In this book, we are talking about another type of person; that is, unethical Manipulators.

* * *

In any given moment, we need to remember the tactics Manipulators use. We will focus on the word D.A.R.K. so you can remember details easily and protect yourself from Manipulators.

D — Dangle something for nothing

A — Alert to scarcity

R — Reveal the Desperate Hot Button

K — Keep on pushing buttons

1. Dangle Something for Nothing

What do conmen and conwomen do to seize your attention? They make you think you're getting a "steal."

I recently saw a documentary in which a conman on a

street in England showed a toy that looked like it was dancing. This fake product was actually dancing because of a hidden, invisible thread. The conman was dangling something for nothing. The Entranced Buyer thought he was getting something worth $20 for only $5. That was the trick. The Entranced Buyer felt that he was getting $15 extra of value for his $5. What the Buyer really got was something worth nothing. Similarly, I know someone who purchased a copy of a Disney movie from a street vendor in San Francisco. She brought the copy home and it was unwatchable—and the street vendor was never seen again.

An old phrase goes, "A conman cannot con someone who is not looking for something for nothing."

How to Protect Yourself from "Dangle Something for Nothing"

Stop! Get on your cell phone and talk through the "deal" with someone you know who thinks clearly. Go home. Think about it. Do some research on the Internet. Listen to your gut feelings. If the salesman or conman is too insistent, get away from that Manipulator. Get quiet. Have a cup of water. Cool down. Break the Trance!

Break the Trance and Identify the Crucial Detail

Earlier, I mentioned that a Manipulator puts you into a trance. An added problem is that we put ourselves into a trance. For example, as you read this, are you thinking about your right toe? Most likely not (unless you stubbed your toe recently). The point is that we only focus on a tiny percentage of what is going on in our life.

Around fifteen years ago, I caused myself trouble because I put myself into a trance. I discovered that under certain conditions, friendship can make you nearly deaf. Here's how: I was producing a song for a motion picture. A good friend was singing backup in the chorus. Because of our friendship, I wanted him to sound great. I completely missed the Crucial Detail. In this kind of situation, the Crucial Detail is that what truly counts is how the lead singer sounds! I made a song that I could not release. What a waste of time and money! I had put myself into a trance.

In any situation in which the Manipulator is "dangling something for nothing," we often fall into a trance and miss the Crucial Detail. The most important detail is *not* that we're saving money if we order before midnight tonight. What counts is whether the product creates a lasting, crucial benefit in our lives. And is the benefit of the product worth the cost? Some people even program themselves to make mistakes by saying, "I can't pass up a bargain." The bargain is *not* the Crucial Detail.

Secrets to Break the Trance
This is the process of B.R.E.A.K.S. It will help you remember the proven methods to break a trance.
B — Breathe
R — Relax
E — Envision
A — Act on aromas
K — Keep moving
S — Smile

Secret #1: Breathe
Remember Secret #1: Manipulators make you hurt and then offer the salve. The Manipulator wants to put you into a state of being that fills you with a sense of urgency and anxiety. Oh, no! I'm going to miss the sale! Stop this highly vulnerable state. Take a deep breath.

End of Excerpt from *Darkest Secrets of Persuasion and Seduction Masters: How to Protect Yourself and Turn the Power to Good*

Purchase your copy of this book (paperback or eBook) at online retailers

See **Free Chapters** of Tom Marcoux's 45 books at http://amzn.to/ZiCTRj

ABOUT THE AUTHOR

You want more and better, right? Imagine fulfilling your Big Dream.

Tom Marcoux can help you—in that he's coached thousands of people: CEOs, small business leaders, graduate students (at Stanford University) speakers, and authors.

Tom is known as an effective **Executive Coach** and **Spoken Word Strategist.**

(and Thought Leader—okay, writing 45 books helped with that!)

*** CEOs, Vice-Presidents, Other Executives, Small Business Leaders:*

You know that leading people and speaking at your best can be tough.

Tom solves problems while helping you amplify *your own Charisma, Confidence, and Control of Time.*

> "Tom Marcoux coached me to get more done in 10 days than other coaches in 2 years."
> – Brad Carlson, CEO of MindStrong LLC

Interested? Email Tom at tomsupercoach@gmail.com Ask for a Special Report: "9 Deadly Mistakes to Avoid for Your Next Speech."

You've heard that you need to tell YOUR STORY well,

right? (We're talking about brand, product, or profile for a job.)

The San Francisco Examiner designated Tom Marcoux as "The Personal Branding Instructor." Why? Tom has helped thousands of clients, audiences, MBA students express their own **powerful Personal Brand.** Tom helps **you communicate powerfully so people trust you** and gain what you're offering (product, service, an idea!).

As a **Pitch Coach,** Marcoux is an expert on STORY. He won a Special Award at the EMMY AWARDS, and he directed a feature film that went to the CANNES FILM MARKET and earned international distribution. Tom founded PitchPowerFest.com (Also see GetTheBigYES.com)

You need to give a great Speech. How about a TED Talk?

"Tom Marcoux has coached me to make my speeches compelling and powerful. He's helping me prepare my TED Talk. Do your career a big favor and engage **Tom Marcoux, the Spoken Word Strategist.**" – Dr. JoAnn Dahlkoetter, author of *Your Performing Edge* and Coach to CEOs and Olympic Gold Medalists

This is YOUR OPPORTUNITY. Apply for a
FREE Breakthrough Strategy Session with Tom
Marcoux at tomsupercoach.com/breakthrough. See the VIDEO.

Tom Marcoux says, "Because of my unique coaching methods, I emphasize with my clients: **You will achieve more than you believe.**"

"Tom helped me unearth deeply emotional and humorous moments in my speech to move the hearts of the audience. He was there for me unconditionally. He went above and beyond anything that I expected. During every interaction that I had with Tom, I felt that I learnt something profound.

I highly recommend for anyone who wants to give a great speech that you work with Tom Marcoux as your Speech Coach and Spoken Word Strategist." – Krishna Noru

As a CEO, Tom leads teams in the United Kingdom, India and the USA. Tom guides clients and audiences (LinkedIn, IBM, Sun Microsystems, etc.) in *Extreme Confidence*, leadership, team-building, power time management and branding.

"Tom Marcoux has been an NAB Conference favorite [speaker] for six years. And he is very energetic." – John Marino, Vice President, National Association of Broadcasters, Washington, D.C.

One of Tom's *Darkest Secrets* books rose to **#1 on Amazon.com Hot New Releases in Business Life** (and in Business Communication). A member of the National Speakers Association for over 17 years, Tom is a professional coach and guest expert on TV, radio, and print.

Tom addressed National Association of Broadcasters' Conference six years in a row. With a degree in psychology, he has presented as a guest lecturer at **Stanford University,** DeAnza College, and California State University. Tom teaches Authentic Leadership Communication & Authentic Marketing at Sofia University, Palo Alto, California. Over the years, Tom has taught business communication, designing careers, public speaking, science fiction/fantasy cinema & literature and comparative religion at Academy of Art University. He is engaged in book/film projects *Crystal*

Pegasus (children's graphic novel) & *Jack AngelSword/Jenalee Storm* (urban fantasy).

Tom provides *A.C.T. Coaching* (Assess, Create, Trim) and *T.O.P. Coaching* (Transform, Optimize, Power-communicate). **With his unique background as a trained feature film director, actor and screenwriter,** Tom will role-play with you so you're ready for the tough meeting and even tougher speech or sales presentation.

> "Using just one of Tom Marcoux's methods, I got more done in 2 weeks than in 6 months." – Jaclyn Freitas, M.A.

Consider Tom Marcoux's well-received Online Course **Get the Big YES: Get More Clients, Express Extreme Confidence and Love Your Business Again** ... send an email to TomSuperCoach@gmail.com

Become a fan of Tom's graphic novels/feature films:

- Urban Fantasy: *Jenalee Storm / Jack AngelSword*
  At Facebook.com type: "JenaleeStorm"

- Science fiction: *TimePulse*
  www.facebook.com/timepulsegraphicnovel

- Children's Fantasy: *Crystal Pegasus*
  www.facebook.com/crystalpegasusandrose

See **Free Chapters** of Tom Marcoux's 45 books—visible at online retailers.

www.ingramcontent.com/pod-product-compliance
Lightning Source LLC
Chambersburg PA
CBHW050106210326
41519CB00015BA/3852